Mental Mathematics for the Numeracy Hour

Tony Harries and Mike Spooner

David Fulton Publishers
London

David Fulton Publishers Ltd
Ormond House, 26–27 Boswell Street, London WC1N 3JD

First published in Great Britain by David Fulton Publishers 2000

Note: The rights of Tony Harries and Mike Spooner to be identified as the authors of this work have been asserted by them in accordance with the Copyright, Designs and Patents Act 1988.

Copyright © Tony Harries and Mike Spooner 2000

British Library Cataloguing in Publication Data
A catalogue record for this book is available from the British Library

ISBN 1–85346–644–1

Typeset by Elite Typesetting Techniques, Eastleigh, Hampshire
Printed in Great Britain by The Cromwell Press Ltd, Trowbridge, Wilts.

Contents

To Graciela, Patrick,
Helen, Paul and Ruth

Preface

We started our careers in education as classroom teachers in primary and secondary schools and were fortunate enough to gain experience both in the UK and abroad. During that time we were able to work, from a school perspective, with students in Initial Teacher Education. Now we work full-time with these students, from a college perspective, as they prepare to start working in schools with children. Our experience has enabled us to see at first hand what we regard as a damaging, wasteful and artificial divide between the exploration of theoretical perspectives through research, which is often thought of as the business of higher education, and the practical enterprise of classroom teaching. We believe strongly that research informs practice and that practice informs research and that this can be a powerful partnership with the potential to enhance classroom practice and hence children's learning experience.

We are both committed to establishing a greater continuity between Initial Teacher Education and Continuing Professional Development and hence between the theoretical and practical issues of teaching and learning. In this book we have sought to offer reviews of relevant research, together with reference points to facilitate further exploration of what we see as the key research issues. We have also included ideas for activities which seek to provide practical solutions for some of the issues raised by the findings of research into children's learning in mathematics and styles of teaching and classroom organisation promoted by the National Numeracy Strategy. The activities have been selected not as ends in themselves but rather as starting points for developing further activity. Our hope is that teachers will find these useful and that they will be able to use and develop them in such a way that their children's learning is enhanced.

Over the years we have been fortunate to work with imaginative colleagues at Bath and inspiring teachers in the schools in the area. To them our thanks. You will recognise many of the activities that we suggest!

Tony Harries (Durham) and Mike Spooner (Bath), December 1999

CHAPTER 1

Introduction

Introduction

What is 75 − 38? How would you approach this calculation? Would you immediately reach for pencil and paper and carry out a standard written algorithm, would you use a mental method such as counting on, or would you work mentally and make jottings of your working as you go along? Do you have any pictures or images in your head as you work? In many ways it doesn't really matter how you approach the calculation since you will have worked out an efficient way of working for yourself. However when we are working with children we want to help them work towards efficient ways of calculating so that they are not prevented from exploring mathematics because their methods of calculation are long and time-consuming activities. In order to do this we need to start with a recognition of pupils' own strategies and work through these towards more efficient ways of working.

It could be argued that all mathematics is a mental activity and that written work is simply an articulation on paper of this activity; this articulation we try to do in as succinct a form as possible. In this book we explore the area of mental mathematics and provide activities which will help teachers develop the mathematical competence and confidence of their pupils and at the same time help pupils to enjoy and value what they are doing.

A number of principles underpin the way in which the book has evolved:

- The *environment or classroom ethos* within which the pupils can develop both their mathematics and themselves as learners, is important. Generally it needs to be both non-competitive and non-judgemental so that pupils can feel confident about taking risks in their exploration of mathematics.

- Pupils need *time* in order to develop their mathematics. They need time to think, time to explore, time to discuss, and time to explain their reasoning.
- Pupils are *constructors* of knowledge and part of the role of the teacher is to 'scaffold' the development of that knowledge and the meaning that the pupils give to the development and application of that knowledge.
- In terms of *progression* this is viewed as a recognition of what the pupils bring with them and the intuitive ways they have of working, and using this to help the pupils work towards more flexible and efficient ways of working.
- Mathematics can be seen as a *mental activity that needs to be communicated*, and as such the pupils need to develop a language they can use in order to facilitate this. The aim will be to develop greater precision and clarity of communication.
- The *National Numeracy Strategy* (NNS) provides a clear framework within which pupils' mathematics can develop. It provides both challenges and support for teachers and needs to be seen as a dynamic framework through which development can occur for both teachers and pupils.

It is probably true that in the past mental mathematics has been perceived as uni-dimensional in that it has been associated with memory tests such as table tests and speed tests – something that for many pupils has been a demoralising and humiliating experience which has created a barrier to the learning of mathematics. In the chapters that follow we try to develop a wider view of mental mathematics which explores the two aspects of mental mathematics identified by Askew (1998) – instant recall (memory activity) and figuring out (strategic activity). In undertaking this task the following themes are explored in a variety of ways.

Variety of approach

The National Numeracy Strategy (DfEE 1999a) has advocated the use of the daily mathematics lesson. In order to make this effective then variety within and across lessons is vital in order that interest and motivation are maintained. Pupils need clear structures within which to work and the daily mathematics lesson will provide this, but within that lesson teachers will need to seek ways in which the pupils remain active and purposeful in their approach to their learning. There are many skills to be developed in the lessons. In addition to technical skills, there are practical skills, investigative skills, and the skill of explanation, to name but a few. Further, the teachers will need to be aware of the increased knowledge about the working of the brain now available and the way in which this knowledge can help us to present ideas to pupils in a way that can be meaningful and appropriate to their way of learning.

Involvement and ethos

In the past, feelings about mathematics among many pupils in schools have been negative. Many students, when asked to talk about their memories and feelings about mathematics, use words such as panic, humiliation, mental multiplication table tests, punishment. It is clear that for them mental mathematics is about short tests – usually of multiplication tables – that depend very much on speed and memory. This has often been a distressing experience for them.

As the NNS is developed in schools it is important that the environment within which the pupils work is positive. Further, it needs to be somewhere where the pupils feel comfortable in addition to being challenged. In developing this kind of ethos within the classroom we need to recognise that working with the whole class is an exercise involving risks to the self-esteem of some pupils. The challenge for the teacher is to create an environment where pupils are prepared to share their thoughts and to see risk-taking as an essential aspect of the learning process (see Figure 1.1).

Figure 1.1

Language and communication

One of the most quoted passages from the Cockcroft Report (1982) is that concerning communication:

> We believe that all these perceptions of the usefulness of mathematics arise from the fact that mathematics provides a means of communication which is powerful, concise and unambiguous. (p. 2)

While the question of ambiguity could be questioned, there can be no argument with the idea that mathematics can be both a powerful and precise way of communicating ideas. Thus we need to be able to help pupils both to develop a language that allows them to talk about mathematics, and also to use mathematical language precisely to explain the solution to problems. Mental mathematics becomes a vehicle through which the linguistic side of mathematics can be developed, as pupils seek ways to explain what they are doing in as precise a way as possible. In the NNS there is a strong emphasis on communication and within this, progression is seen as the development of greater precision.

Developing skills which underpin calculation

In *The National Numeracy Strategy* (DfEE 1999a) a number of skills of calculation are identified. These skills are underpinned by:

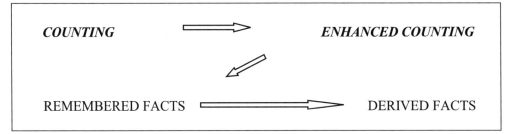

COUNTING   *ENHANCED COUNTING*

REMEMBERED FACTS   DERIVED FACTS

Figure 1.2

- Some number facts need to be *remembered* so that there can be instant recall without hesitation. These will include addition/subtraction facts as well as multiplication/division facts. The number of these facts that the pupils need to know will develop from year to year but there can be no doubt that having a set of remembered facts is an advantage in pursuing efficient methods of calculation.
- Some strategies *make use of known facts* in order to complete other calculations. These will include an understanding that knowing a single digit addition fact will enable other calculations to be undertaken speedily. For example knowing $5 + 7 = 12$ facilitates the calculation of $50 + 70$, $35 + 7$ ... $12 - 7$, $120 - 70$ ... Similarly, knowing a simple multiplication fact enables other calculations to be undertaken. For example, knowing that $6 \times 2 = 12$ facilitates the calculation of 60×2, 6×20, 600×2 ... 6×4, 6×8 ... $12 \div 2$, $120 \div 2$ ...

This second skill requires the pupils to be able to look at a number and/or a calculation and to use their knowledge of the structure of the number system to identify related calculations. It also means that it is important for pupils to be able to look at numbers and see through them so that the richness of the number is appreciated and used.

Competence and efficiency

In working with numbers our objective has to be the ability to calculate both competently and efficiently. In pursuing this, much research (Bierhoff 1996, Gravemeijer 1994) and observation of practice in other countries suggests that working mentally and not rushing into formal written methods is important. This does not suggest that mental and written methods are unconnected, but that confidence and competence with mental methods will actually help in understanding formal written methods. Often when doing mental calculations pupils will need to make informal jottings both to help their progress and to remind them of what they have done. There are two ways of looking at the mental/written methods interface. One is to see it as a progression or a link – a formal, succinct way of efficiently expressing on paper approximately what was being followed 'in head'. The other is to see it as a switch – that a formal written method is an alternative way of performing a calculation which in some circumstances is more efficient. Recognising whether, for them, the methods are linked or alternative is important for pupils.

Developing links

In the King's College study (Askew *et al.* 1997) which explored effective teaching of numeracy, the researchers concluded that numeracy teaching was most effectively undertaken by teachers who saw connections in mathematics and sought to help pupils to see the connections and so become efficient workers with numbers. It is thus important that when pupils learn a fact they are also able to give related facts which can also be 'known'. For example, the idea of linking addition and subtraction is crucial in developing efficiency so that pupils know that once they know a fact such as $5 + 7 = 12$, then they also know that $12 - 7 = 5$, $12 - 5 = 7$ and $7 + 5 = 12$. In this way one known fact becomes four known facts. Similarly with multiplication and division, knowing one fact such as $6 \times 4 = 24$ immediately becomes four known facts with $4 \times 6 = 24$, $24 \div 4 = 6$, $24 \div 6 = 4$ added to the original one.

The idea about connections goes further with clear links being made between addition and multiplication and between subtraction and division. In this way the whole of mathematical calculation becomes a series of interconnecting activities rather than disconnected ones.

Creating images

One way in which pupils can be helped to progress efficiently and competently with their calculations is through the images that are used to 'scaffold' their development. This idea of scaffolding will be addressed in Chapter 2. These images are broadly of three types.

- Firstly we have *sound* images. When young children are learning anything involving words they will keep repeating the word until it sounds right. Similarly with pupils working with number they will work on counting until the sequence they are using sounds right. Thus with young children the use of rhymes will be an important activity which focuses attention on the sound of the words or sequences.
- Secondly there are *concrete* images which are broadly of two types which are linked to seeing and touching. In this way the learner can link sound to either/both something they can see and/or something that they can touch. The most commonly used resources for this are beads and blocks.
- Finally there are the *symbolic* images which are the mathematical symbols which the pupils need to know and which are the symbolic representations of the sound, sight and touch images with which they are familiar. These are the symbols which they will then need to learn to manipulate in order to develop their mathematical competence.

It should be noted that although the images are listed sequentially it is not a hierarchical sequence. The pupils need to be able to move confidently between images and not feel the need to leave one type of image behind when they 'move on'.

The structure of the book

We believe that good practice in the classroom needs to be underpinned by an understanding of the theories about the way in which children learn mathematics. Thus the second chapter explores the development of theories about the learning of mathematics and seeks to place the role of mental mathematics within that context. The chapter stresses the need to move from the uni-dimensional view of mental mathematics which emphasises the recall of number facts to explore present day understandings of the multi-dimensional aspects of working in one's head. It also explores the way in which the development of mental strategies helps in the understanding of concepts and aids the development of written methods.

Chapters 3 to 6 focus on particular themes within mental mathematics and will follow the same format. A brief review of research on the theme of the chapter is followed where appropriate by a consideration of the curriculum and classroom management issues related to the theme. The last part of the chapter consists of a set of activities which illustrate the theme of the chapter and can be used with children at different stages in their schooling, or as INSET activities with teachers.

Chapter 3 focuses on the development of a classroom ethos for mental mathematics. Initially the research in this area is outlined and discussed – providing a rationale for the activities that follow. Here there is a strong emphasis on involvement activities, using such resources as flashback cards and number petals as devices for involvement.

Chapter 4 focuses on mathematical images, describing the images that we would expect children to relate to at different stages in their schooling, and exploring some of the idiosyncratic images that children develop for themselves. This chapter concentrates on addition and subtraction. The chapter then introduces activities for each year group which would help children both to develop and to use these images in their numeracy work.

Chapter 5 focuses on the way that mathematical ideas/concepts are represented. In particular the chapter concentrates on the operations of multiplication and division. The activities in the chapter focus on tasks for each year group that help children to use and develop competence in the use of a variety of representations which aid the development of numerical competence.

Chapter 6 focuses on aspects of using and applying mathematics within mental mathematics. Here issues related to language and communication are important and the chapter contains ideas about communication activities that can be used effectively with children.

Chapter 7 contains a range of supporting activities. In particular there is a consideration of non-numerical aspects of mental mathematics. The activities in this chapter include a range of open-ended tasks.

CHAPTER 2

Perspectives on the teaching and learning of mathematics

Introduction

The purpose of this book is to explore the various aspects of mental mathematics and to gain some realisation of how mental mathematics underpins the development of an understanding of many mathematical concepts. In this chapter we introduce a brief survey of some of the main theories related to the teaching and learning of mathematics. As the theories are reviewed comments will be made on the effect that the different theories have had on the way in which learning in schools has developed.

The view taken throughout this book is that learning is an active process which affects behaviour in a more or less permanent way. Clearly learning takes place from the moment a child is born and is the result of various influences and stimuli. These influences and stimuli provide the impetus for mental activity. We recognise that this applies both out of school and in school and that much learning takes place in the first few years of a child's life, long before they start formal schooling. But for the purpose of this book we are concerned with the development of pupils' mental mathematics that can be stimulated and developed through activities that take place within the school environment. First we will think a little about mental mathematics and then we will survey the various theories on learning.

Mental mathematics

What images do the words 'mental mathematics' conjure up in your head? When we ask our students to talk about some of their memories of mathematics it is very often mental mathematics that they recall. The words conjure up memories of tables tests, quick-fire sets of sums, the expectation of instant recall and unfortunately feelings of fear and humiliation. It is rarely associated with learning! Surprisingly, despite all the talk about the importance of mental mathematics it is difficult to find a really clear definition of what we mean.

In *Mathematics Teaching* (MT) *160* (ATM 1997) the editors used an e-mail that they were sent from a Grayson Wheatley of Florida State University (p. 21). In this he says that:

> Mental mathematics is redundancy. Since mathematics is purely abstract, mathematical activity is necessarily mental. Yes we record our symbolisation at times to assist our reasoning but the mathematics occurs in the head not on paper ... Mental mathematics ... is the only mathematics that exists.

A strong statement which clearly has some truth in it. Mental mathematics is not about just memory. It is about the way we think mathematically and for it to be meaningful what we write needs to express what we are thinking. So the challenge for us as teachers is to seek ways in which we can facilitate and develop this process in our pupils. This gives a much broader feel to mental mathematics than the original pilot tests on mental arithmetic which stated that they were designed to assess 'mental recall and agility when dealing with numerical problems'.

Of course mental mathematics is not just about number work. It is about working mentally in all areas of mathematics. In number work we want children to know some facts and to be able to use those known facts to perform other calculations – the development of appropriate strategies for calculation. What would we mean by mental geometry or mental algebra? Again in *MT 160*, which was devoted almost entirely to considering aspects of mental mathematics, David Feilker (1997) explores this question. You might like to try these two activities and then reflect on how you worked:

Activity 1.

- Slice a proportion off each corner of a cube in an obviously symmetrical way.
- Continue slicing until all edges meet at the mid points of the edges of the cube.
- Continue a little further.
- Continue until all the edges are equal.
- Continue until all the slices meet at the centres of the faces of the cube.
- Continue.

How did you work? Did you imagine a cube and imagine making the cuts? Would you have liked to have had a cube in front of you? Did you make any conjectures and try to prove them by visualising what was happening? Did you focus on one corner? Was it hard trying to make sense of the words with no picture to help?

Activity 2.

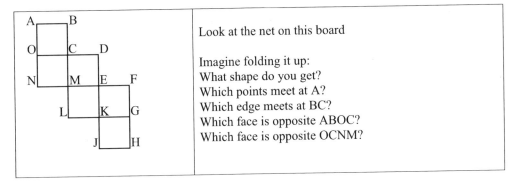

A, B, O, C, D, N, M, E, F, L, K, G, J, H	Look at the net on this board Imagine folding it up: What shape do you get? Which points meet at A? Which edge meets at BC? Which face is opposite ABOC? Which face is opposite OCNM?

Figure 2.1

What difference did it make this time when there was a picture available with which to work? Did it help? If so, how did it help you to work on the problem?

David Feilker also talks about mental algebra. He illustrates this by considering the total number of diagonals of a seven-sided figure. This could be done by simply drawing all the diagonals and counting them or we could look at the way in which we could organise the count. For example, we could ask:

- How many diagonals from one vertex?
- Is this true for all vertices?
- Can I now just multiply the number of vertices by the number of diagonals from one vertex?
- What about double counting?
- Does this help me to work out the number of diagonals in any polygon?

In other words, can I generalise? (which is the essence of algebra).

So there are many ways of working mentally in mathematics and in all cases we use a variety of representations in order to help us to proceed. They may be pictures, diagrams, physical movements, etc. The different representations that we can use will be the focus of the following chapters and the activities used are designed to help the pupils become familiar with and confident in using a variety of representations. They will then be able to choose appropriate representations for problems that they face.

However, before delving further into aspects of mental mathematics we feel that it is important to have a broad view of various learning theories into which ideas about mental mathematics might fit. We end the chapter with a few comments on representation of mathematical ideas.

Drill and practice theories

One of the first theories about how children learn was developed by Thorndike and Skinner (cited in MacDonald 1964). This theory was described as the 'Stimulus – Response' Theory. Thorndike's view of learning was that it was about developing connections and that these connections were a means whereby behaviour could be modified. His work suggested two educational principles:

Put together what should go together and keep apart what should not go together.
Reward desirable connections and make undesirable connections produce discomfort. (MacDonald 1964, p. 8)

Much of his theory was developed from experiments which were similar to those carried out by Pavlov in Russia. From the experiments Thorndike developed his Law of Effect which stated that 'behaviour which is followed by reward or success will tend to be repeated whereas behaviour which is not rewarded will tend to die away' (MacDonald 1964). It was this law which Thorndike applied to the teaching of mathematics (in particular arithmetic), developing the principle of 'drill and practice'. The object being that, when pupils were presented with the stimulus '2 + 2', they would come up with the response '4'. His belief was that arithmetic consisted of a countless set of bonds or connections and that it was the role of the teacher to enable pupils to know these bonds.

These principles had implications for the teaching of mathematics – the learning of mathematics was imposed from outside the learner, someone else decided the connections and their related rewards and discomforts, and the connections were perceived to be the same for all learners. The system was very much grounded in memory and written methods – little attention seemed to be given to what was going on in the heads of the learners. This naturally led to the idea of individualised programmed learning as the key to progress, on the grounds that while the connections necessary to facilitate learning were the same, the rate at which the connections may be assimilated would be different for different learners. It could be hypothesised that learning was equated to training within this theory.

It is also possible that Thorndike's ideas were greatly influenced by the needs of the era in which he operated (the early part of the twentieth century) and also the tools for learning that were available at the time. There was a need for paper and pencil accuracy in the performance of a range of 'sums'. It was not a universal necessity but a necessity for an educated group. It could be that, given these circumstances, his theory represented an efficient framework for the development of appropriate competence. But there are difficulties with his theories. He appears to take little or no account of the 'process' which may be considered to be the mediator between the stimulus and the response, and of course this mediator can vary greatly between pupils. Also, he makes no distinction between doing and understanding. His view of mathematics was a clinical one and took no account of who the learner was and why they might wish to learn the correct response to countless stimuli.

Two important schools of psychological thought developed at about the same time as Thorndike – but took very different views of learning – Dewey and Gestalt. The views of Dewey are significant in that they question a number of the 'Thorndike principles'. Firstly, he questioned the view that stimuli needed to be externally produced. He suggested that the stimulus was directly related to the learner, his or her experience and his or her environment, and that the response to the stimulus resulted in new stimuli. Thus the notion of a linear system of discrete stimulus – response situations organised externally was replaced by a stimulus–response circuit in which the learner was an active participant. Secondly, Dewey was also concerned about the interest and motivation of the learner, believing that this was an important factor in ensuring that learning was a positive experience. Thirdly, he believed that there must be an *aim* in learning and that it must involve a personal aim and not just one imposed from outside. It is a clear aim combined with interest and motivation which produces intelligent action. MacDonald (1964) summarises Dewey's view on learning as:

> problem-solving or intelligent action in which the person continually evaluates his/her experience in the light of its foreseen and experienced consequences ... learning in this sense is not simply an acquisition or achievement but a moment of experience out of which emerges redefined purposes, new evaluations, and new actions in the service of continued growth. (p. 13)

Thus for Dewey learning was not a clinical exercise but something which was deeply rooted in personal development. It was something in which the learner was an active participator and was clearly grounded in mental activity.

The Gestalt psychologists added two important points to Dewey's thoughts (see Resnick and Ford 1981). Firstly, they reacted very strongly against the idea that learning was something which was broken down into its constituent parts and then the learner learnt each of these constituent parts without having a view of wholeness. They believed that the significance of a situation or pattern of stimuli is in the total pattern and not in its separate elements (Stones 1966). This links closely with Dewey's ideas about learning and problem-solving, as solving a problem is not about working blindly on the constituent parts of the problem, but working on the constituent parts because they are directly related to a vision of the whole problem.

Secondly, they believed that insight played a part in learning and problem-solving, and that insight was directly related to having a 'whole' view of a problem.

These schools of thought led to a quite different view about how learning might best be facilitated in school. Whereas Thorndike took the view that all the small bits of learning would eventually constitute a whole when the myriad connections were understood, both Dewey and the Gestalt psychologists sought to put learning in a context. This allowed the learner to have a view of the whole problem first and then to see the bits as a way of making sense of the whole.

Theories of development – Piaget

Piaget (1969) rejected Thorndike's theory of learning which was based on the idea of stimulus–response. He maintained that rather than think of stimulus–response as a linear process of external stimulus invoking personal response, it should be thought of as a feedback loop, in that response can affect stimulus and thus it is not a one-way schema.

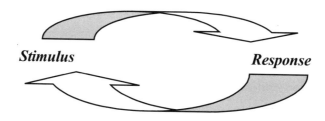

Stimulus   *Response*

Figure 2.2

Piaget placed active involvement in personally meaningful problem-solving at the centre of learning and development with three basic principles being central to his theory. Firstly, there is *assimilation*. At any stage of development the individual has a mental conceptual structure. When he or she receives new information or has a new experience, that experience has to fit into these existing structures. Secondly, there is *accommodation*, which is understood as the restructuring of existing mental structures in order to accommodate a new experience. For example, the child who has developed an understanding of '5' has to expand that understanding in order to make sense of '54'. Sometimes the accommodation will involve minor adjustments to mental structures whereas at other times the adjustments can be quite dramatic. Thirdly, there is *equilibration*, which is the process whereby conflicting ideas are harmonised. For example, the notion that the symbol '5' has a unique meaning is upset by the numbers '54', '564', '0.5'. The mental conflict has to be harmonised by some concept of place value, and an *internalisation* of the idea that the symbol '5' has 'context-related' meaning.

These principles underlie the development of Piaget's stages of development. He postulated that learning was subordinate to development and that there were four stages or periods of development through which all children passed.

The first stage he termed the *sensory-motor stage* (birth to eighteen months). This is the stage of actions – both reflex and 'learned' – and sensations associated with the actions. During this stage the child develops habits that produce pleasing sensations. He or she develops a sense of permanence – that is objects exist even when they cannot be seen. He or she starts to set simple objectives and develop a plan for achieving the objective. Also he or she starts to develop the concept of *physical reversibility* or *inverse operations,* e.g. dropping and picking up, putting a spoon in a bowl and taking it out.

The second stage he termed the *pre-operation stage* (eighteen months to four years). During this stage the child starts to develop the power of *representation.* Words are used to represent objects, blocks are used to represent various objects from cars to towers, and he or she starts to draw representational pictures. For most of this stage Piaget argues that a child is only able to centre on one aspect of an experience. Thus for most children of this age they would say that a tall glass would hold more liquid than a short glass – irrespective of the other dimensions of the glass. They focus only on the height of the glass and make their judgements based on that.

The third stage he termed *concrete operational* (seven to twelve years). This is the stage during which the child develops what Piaget calls 'logico-mathematical thought' and starts to think operationally with the help of physical manipulation of objects. He or she continues to develop an understanding of *reversibility*, in that now he or she may be able to argue that since 2 + 7 = 9 then 9 – 2 = 7. Ideas about conservation and invariance become firmly rooted, so that children can now centre on more than one aspect of an experience and so understand for themselves that in the flower and vase experiment (see Rosnick and Ford 1981) the number of flowers and the number of vases are the same. Also Piaget believed that it is at this stage that children start to develop such logical principles as *transitivity* so that they can argue that if A > B and B > C then A > C.

The fourth stage he termed *formal operations* (twelve years onwards). In this stage Piaget claims that children develop the ability to make hypotheses, generalise an argument and make logical deductions.

There are a number of points that need to be made about Piaget's theories. Firstly, it must be emphasised that the theory is about development and not about learning. As Davis (1991, p. 22) says,

> Piaget had little to say about the educational implications of his work, and where he did comment it was not necessarily in a way that shed a very positive light on the teaching profession … Development is seen as gradual changes

reflected in stages; learning is more specific and determined by the stages themselves.

Thus he makes no comment on the way in which learning may influence development.

Secondly (and this is closely related to the first point) he rejects the idea that development can be accelerated. He calls it an American obsession and he suggests that it may be possible to accelerate learning, but the best time will depend on each individual and the area being studied.

Thirdly, and possibly most importantly, he pays little attention to the role of language in development. He held that language was a reflector of cognitive achievement rather than a controller of it. This lack of attention to language has led researchers to question the validity of some of Piaget's important experiments. In questioning one of Piaget's experiments – the conservation experiment where children were shown a glass of water which was then poured into glasses of different sizes/shapes, and the children were asked each time if the new glass contained the same amount of water – Bruner claimed that 'perceptual seduction' prevented the children from saying that there was the same amount of water in each glass. In other words a visual perception dominated their thinking. Thus Bruner (1964, 1970) redesigned Piaget's experiment into four stages:

1. Do Piaget's original experiment in order to classify the children as conservers or non-conservers.
2. Repeat the experiment with the first glass visible to the child but all other glasses hidden behind a screen.
3. Repeat the experiment with all glasses visible to the child, and ask the child to predict the level of water that will occur in the glasses which were previously hidden.
4. Repeat Piaget's experiment.

The results of this work showed a quite remarkable increase in the percentage of 'conservers' among the children and so suggested to Bruner that the concept of conservation could be developed through appropriate instruction. The results of Bruner's conservation experiment are listed below:

Ages of children (in years)		4	5	6	7
Percentage of conservers	Before teaching	0	20	50	50
	After teaching	0	75	90	90

It would appear from this that the 4-year-olds were unaffected by Bruner's instruction sequence, whereas the 5-, 6- and 7-year olds were positively affected to varying degrees. This could imply more than just effective instruction but could imply the idea of an 'optimum input period', i.e. if children are instructed or guided at the most appropriate time and in the most appropriate way then they can learn at speed. A key to Bruner's work is the resources with which he encourages the pupils to think. This idea of resources or more appropriately 'tools to think with' will be taken up in later chapters.

Clearly the work of Piaget has been very influential in the development of ideas about the learning of mathematics. In some ways it has encouraged the development of the idea of readiness for learning particular concepts. This can then be used as a reason for pupils not being able to learn something, since Piaget's theories suggest that certain learning can only take place when the appropriate development stage has been reached. This is clearly not the only possibility for a child who is not learning. It could be that the tools with which the pupil is being expected to think are not appropriate for that child. Further, it could be that the contextual situation in which they are pursuing the learning is not appropriate.

There can be no question about the influence of Piaget's work but, as indicated, his work would appear to be more concerned with developmental structure than learning. His concern with stages of development did not include work on the process whereby the learner progressed from one stage to another. This is why language and social interaction played little part in Piaget's work. In considering theories of learning, the work of Bruner and Vygotsky are considered in some detail.

Developing theories of learning – Bruner

The main concern of Bruner was to do with learning processes – particularly those associated with creative problem-solving. Thus he was deeply concerned with the way in which language, communication and instruction affected the development of knowledge and understanding (Wood 1988). One of his claims was that: 'Any idea or body of knowledge can be presented in a form simple enough so that any particular learner can understand it' (Bruner 1964, p. 44). This was a claim which was seriously questioned by Piaget who described it as 'astounding', and while he did accept that in some circumstances it may be possible to accelerate learning he did not believe that Bruner's suggestion was ever desirable.

Bruner (1964) postulated that a theory of instruction has four main features. Firstly, a theory of instruction should specify the experiences which most effectively implant in the individual a predisposition to learning. This fits closely with Dewey's ideas on the importance of motivation in learning. However, Bruner takes the idea beyond that of motivation and suggests that learning and problem-solving depend upon the three aspects of 'exploration of alternatives'. These are *activation* which simply means that tasks need to be sufficiently open as to arouse curiosity, a term which Howe (1992) uses often in his work with high-achieving pupils, but not so open as to arouse confusion; *maintenance* which means that the pursuit of alternatives is considered useful and worthwhile; and *direction* which means keeping in mind a view of the whole problem (a Gestaltian principle) and alternative means of achieving a solution to the problem.

Secondly, a theory of instruction must specify ways in which a body of knowledge should be structured so that it can be grasped readily by the learner. Again there were three aspects to this principle. The most important is the mode of presentation, and the three which he suggests could be said to be compatible with Piaget's levels of development. The *enactive* mode concerns the representation of a concept by means of actions. For example, a young child can experience the principle of balancing by playing games on a see-saw. The *iconic* mode concerns the representation of concepts through pictures, graphics or images. So that in this mode the child could experience balancing by working with a model of a balance beam. The *symbolic* mode is where the concept is represented in some abstract symbolic form. This would correspond to experiencing the principles of balancing through a written description or mathematical formula.

The other aspects of this feature were economy – which simply means that the learner should receive the optimum amount of information to be processed (too little will frustrate, and too much will confuse) – and power – which means that the learner must be empowered by what they learn to move ever onwards.

Thirdly, a theory of instruction should specify the most effective sequences in which to present the materials to be learnt. While Bruner does not advocate one prescribed sequence for all children he does suggest that the sequencing should take into account the three modes of presentation. He accepts that if a child has a highly developed sense of symbolism, then the enactive and iconic modes could be bypassed. However, these modes should be available as a 'fall-back' in cases where the symbolic representation has not brought about the desired level of understanding. He also suggests that sequencing is not a linear process but more a spiral one where concepts are visited many times but with increased linguistic precision each time.

Lastly, a theory of instruction should specify the nature and pacing of rewards and punishments in the process of learning. Children need to have a clear goal so that they always know where their work is leading them. They need to be empowered to know what they are able to do with their new knowledge. This is a means of achieving personal satisfaction. If learning is proceeding in a particular mode then any corrective work needs to be delivered in the same mode. All this is aimed at making the learner self-sufficient. This idea of self-sufficiency and empowerment is returned to later when ideas related to the representation of mathematics are discussed.

Two important points that Bruner makes are:

The theory of instruction seeks to take account of the fact that the curriculum reflects not only the nature of knowledge, but also the nature of the knower and the knowledge-getting process. (Bruner 1964, p. 334)

So, as with Piaget, he emphasises the importance of the individual in considering the learning process.

To instruct someone in these disciplines (bodies of knowledge) is not to get him to commit to mind. Rather it is to teach him to participate in the process that makes possible the establishment of knowledge. We teach a subject not to produce living libraries on the subject but rather to get a student to think mathematically for himself, to consider matters as a historian does, to embody the process of knowledge-getting. Knowing is a process not a product. (Bruner 1964, p. 335)

These ideas have been developed further in Wood (1988), where he discusses the development of contingent teaching 'which helps pupils to develop local expertise' (p. 80). The process involves starting with a task and then helping the pupils to break it down into a sequence of smaller and manageable tasks. In order to facilitate this the amount of help given is carefully managed so that a lack of understanding will result in more help, whereas understanding will result in the teacher taking a more withdrawn role. He suggests that in this way the learner is 'never left alone when he is in difficulty nor is he held back by teaching that is too directive and intrusive' (p. 81). He terms this system of help for the learner 'scaffolding' and suggests that used correctly it allows the learner to 'achieve heights that they cannot scale alone' (p. 80). Questions which arise from this work are:

- Who decides how the initial task is to be broken down into smaller tasks?
- Is the ultimate aim for the learner to be able to manage the breaking up of the initial task?
- Can all tasks be considered in this way or is it only applicable to tasks that have a clearly defined structure?
- If that is true how could the same principles be applied to other tasks?

The question that arises for us in this book is, what mathematical tools and representations can we use in order to develop pupils' mental mathematics? In other words, how do the tools that are available for use by the learner affect the possible ways in which mental activity can be pursued?

Two levels of learning – Vygotsky

Although chronologically Vygotsky's work precedes that of Bruner it seems appropriate to consider his work at this point, and to consider the extra dimension which Bruner did not develop. Vygotsky placed instruction at the heart of human learning and development. He starts with the child and his or her own active involvement in learning for development. He strongly believed that communication and social interaction were prerequisites for learning:

> Children confronted with a problem that is slightly too complicated for them exhibit a complex variety of responses including direct attempts at attaining the goal, the use of tools, speech directed toward the person conducting the experiment or speech that simply accompanies the action.... From the very first days of the child's development his activities acquire a meaning of their own in a system of social behaviour and, being directed towards a definitive purpose, are refracted through the prism of the child's environment. The path from object to child and from child to object passes through another person. This complex human structure is the product of a developmental process deeply rooted in the links between individual and social history. (Vygotsky 1978, p. 30)

This illustrates one of the fundamental differences between Piaget and Vygotsky. While Piaget saw development almost entirely in terms of biology, Vygotsky saw it as the result of a link between biology and environmental interaction. In fact he believed in a dual stage process of internalisation.

> Every function in the child's cultural development appears twice: first on the social level, and later, on the individual level; first, between people (interpsychological), and then inside the child (intrapsychological). This applies equally to voluntary attention, to logical memory and to the formation of concepts. All the higher functions originate as actual relations between human individuals. (Vygotsky 1978, p. 57)

This view bears some similarity with Piaget's thoughts on equilibrium. In both cases they are concerned with the way in which children internalise knowledge – the process whereby mental structures are adapted in order that sense is made of new knowledge or information. But whereas Piaget believed that the process was a personal and individual one, Vygotsky interpreted the process in a wider sense and recognised the role of external and social forces in this process.

Vygotsky considered two levels of performance. These were *unassisted performance* (which is what Piaget worked on) and *assisted performance* which is investigating what the child does with assistance. Thus he distinguishes between a child's learning level and his or her developmental level. He justifiably postulates that the learning level is higher than the developmental level, and the gap between the two levels he terms the *Zone of Proximal Development*:

> It is the distance between the actual developmental level as determined by independent problem solving and the level of potential development as determined through problem solving under adult guidance or in collaboration with more capable peers ... the Zone of Proximal Development defines those functions that have not yet matured ... These functions could be termed the 'buds' or 'flowers' of development rather than the fruits of development. (Vygotsky 1978, p. 86)

Thus Vygotsky maintains that for any 'domain of skill' a Zone of Proximal Development can be created which will vary for individuals and within cultures, and from his thinking he defines good teaching as that which 'awakens and arouses to life those functions which are in a stage of maturing' (p. 90). Learning takes place when 'assistance is offered at points in the Zone of Proximal Development at which performance requires assistance'. Learning is dependent on the right kind of social interaction.

In discussing Vygotsky's ideas, Tharp and Gallimore (1991, p. 48ff) suggest four stages of the Zone of Proximal Development. At the start of the first stage which they term 'where performance is assisted by more capable others' the child has little if any understanding of the task and so is dependent on outside stimulus or help. The help will be directive and the child will often copy actions or simply follow directions until, through conversation and action, a notion of the overall task dawns. Meaning appears to be established. This is the process that Wood (1988) has called scaffolding. This process

> breaks down the task into a sequence of smaller tasks which children can manage to perform, and orchestrates the sequence so that they eventually manage to construct the completed assembly ... Built well, such scaffolds help children to scale heights that they cannot scale alone. (Wood 1988, p. 80)

The important feature of scaffolding is not just that it is an attractive metaphor giving images of breadth and depth, and alternative routes to the same location, but that it does not lose sight of the whole task. The 'sequence of smaller tasks' is always seen as part of the whole. In discussing this stage Wood uses the term 'contingent questioning' to define the kind of input which is sensitive to the needs of the child, so that lack of understanding receives more help while understanding enables the teacher to step back. In his study with a group of mothers, he found that while it was a relatively easy idea to understand, it was more difficult to put into operation than expected. To give the correct amount of help at the correct time demanded a great deal of skill.

The next stage is when the child has become his or her own assistant, and so starts to direct their own activities. From the first stage they have learnt the kinds of questions to ask and the strategies to employ. Thus control is being internalised. Wood suggests that during this stage the child will often be talking to himself or herself and is taking on the role of the child and the 'capable other'.

The third stage is where the child moves into the development stage of the task. Thus the task can be executed with ease or has been 'automatised'.

The fourth stage recognises the fact that learning is not a simple linear process but a rather more complex process. There will be times when the child loses the ability to perform a task with ease. He or she has been de-automatised and so will need to go back through the appropriate stages of the Zone of Proximal Development in order to regain the state of automatisation.

The purpose of this structure is to help children to make sense of and gain some understanding of the world in which they live, and to help them to understand the way of thinking in different disciplines. As Wood writes:

> Unless the child practises the role of being a mathematician, historian or geographer, learns the issues that excite people, the problems that interest them and the tools that help them to resolve and solve these, then the child may only learn empty tricks or procedures and will not inherit the discipline itself. (Wood 1988, p. 84)

A constructivist perspective

The struggle over the last half century seems to be to gain an understanding of cognitive development, teaching and learning, and the relation, if any, between them. In analysing the schools of thought it would seem that as Vygotsky (1978) suggests there are three alternatives. The Thorndike School seems to equate learning with development. Piaget and the exponents of his theories would seem to belong to a school which sees learning and development as separate – development happens anyway. Learning may take place at each stage of development but does not influence the developmental level. The third school is the one to which Bruner and Vygotsky would belong – a school which tries to bring learning and development into a 'whole' theory. Learning is an element of environmental stimulus which pushes forward maturation, which in turn stimulates more learning and results in development. Theories are then developed on ways of maximising learning. These theories develop the notion of Zone of Proximal Development and scaffolding. Both are powerful notions for recognising the role of external influences in helping children to construct their own understanding of mathematics.

The next stage in this review of the development of research on the way children learn is to investigate how theories of learning fit in with what is currently called *constructivism*. There are similarities as illustrated by von Glaserfeld's two principles (1995):

Knowledge is not passively received but built up by the cognising subject.

The function of cognition is adaptive and serves the organisation of the experimental world not the discovery of ontological reality. (p.18)

The first produces no real problems as action underpins the work of Piaget, Bruner and Vygotsky. However the second needs some expansion, as it would seem that, while Bruner and Vygotsky would both agree that instruction is a means whereby one is helped to organise knowledge in order to help one make sense of the world, it would also appear that it is a means whereby the learner is challenged to make sense of the 'not known' and to bring it into the mind of the learner. From Piaget onwards two keywords stand out – problem-solving and action. It is these that need to be the foundation, so that the child becomes a genuine participator not a spectator, so that a scaffold is constructed by the teacher which ensures that 'the child's ineptitudes can be rescued by appropriate intervention', and so that the scaffold can be removed part by part as the reciprocal structure is able to stand by itself (Bruner 1983, quoted in Light *et al.* 1991, p. 109).

Constructivism and mathematics education

Modern ideas about constructivism need to be considered in two parts – *radical constructivism* which emanates from the ideas of Piaget and *social constructivism* which emanates from the work of Vygotsky. The principles which underpin the various aspects of constructivism are outlined by Ollerenshaw and Ritchie (1993) as:

- what is already in the learner's mind matters;
- individuals construct their own meaning;
- the construction of meaning is a continuous and active process;
- learning may involve conceptual change;
- the construction of meaning does not always lead to belief;
- learners have final responsibility for their learning;
- some constructed meanings are shared.

There is little to disagree with in these statements which are really self-evident. Clearly what is in the learner's mind matters – if false assumptions are made about prior knowledge then misunderstandings can easily arise. Again, it is clear that in the end an individual must construct their own meaning but the teaching and learning process that they go through can hinder or aid that process. The third point is an important one to recognise as there is often an assumption in mathematics that meaning is fixed. It needs to be recognised that meaning is often domain-specific and that as the domain within which the learner works changes then meaning may also be transformed. This is what leads to the conceptual change that is considered as the fourth point. The idea about meaning leading to belief is also an important one since it is a meaningful belief which provides the firm foundation on which learning can be built. The final point emphasises the fact that, while the individual does need to construct their own meaning, part of the process of doing this involves the learner in sharing meaning and communicating their beliefs. In summary, learning is an activity pursued by the learner and therefore from a psychological point of view he or she can do none other than become actively involved in giving meaning to his or her own learning whatever style of teaching the learner is exposed to.

The essence of constructivism

In considering the nature of constructivism, Cobb *et al.* (1992) consider it to be an alternative to a 'representational view of mind in mathematics education'. This sees learning as a process in which students work on their internal representations so that they mirror the external representations to which the student is exposed. Thus, working with Diennes blocks or Cuisenaire rods is an external representation which the student is expected to use in order to give meaning through some form of internal representation to place value. The difficulty is that the purveyor of the external representation already has an internal representation to which he or she relates the external representation. The student only has the external representation through which meaning is to be developed. Constructivists suggest that this is an extremely difficult thing to achieve and that we must seek ways of helping the learner to construct meaning through their own individual effort. The learning of the student needs to be more openly active rather than hidden behind the illusory façade of the passive recipient.

Cobb *et al.* suggest that the difficulty with the representational approach is that it depends to a large extent on the expert interpretation of the teacher and not on the constructing power of the student. The representational view locates the source of meaning outside the student whereas the constructivist approach locates the meaning within the student and his or her environment. The representational view appears to set up a dualistic conflict within the student between 'in head' or internal representations and external ones which are located in the environment, whereas the constructivist approach would seek to start with the internal representations and seek ways in which they can be externalised and then modified. Further there is the assumption that specific mathematical meaning is actually present in the external representation. This is true for the presenter but not necessarily for the receiver. Finally, Cobb suggests that a representational view of the learning of mathematics encourages the learner to separate school mathematics from mathematics in other settings. These concerns lead Cobb to suggest that: 'we should attempt to develop instructional situations in which the teacher can draw on students, prior experiences to guide the negotiation of initial conventions of interpretation' (p. 13) and that this leads to the view that: 'the learning teaching process commences from the students' initial mathematizations of hypothetical situations described in instructional activities' (p. 13).

This gives a clear starting point for mathematical activity with pupils but it is also necessary to have a clear view as to what the learner is aiming for.

Radical constructivism

This was a theory developed by von Glaserfeld (1987) and others and is encapsulated by the two principles stated above. He suggests that his theory is radical because 'it breaks with convention and develops a theory of knowledge that does not reflect an objective ontological reality, but exclusively an ordering and organising of a world constituted by our experience' (p. 216).

He considers two forms of knowledge, the first is an iconic conception of knowledge which requires a match or correspondence between the cognitive structures and what the structures are supposed to represent. Truth becomes a perfect match between the structures and the representation. This view of knowledge is considered to be derived from a behaviourist view in which observable stimuli and observable responses are 'all that matters'. The second view of knowledge is that which human reason derives from experience. It is the knowledge that fits observations. This is developed from the Piagetian view that knowledge is operative not figurative. In other words, it is actually constructed by the individual. This view of knowledge moves from the view that in order to develop knowledge the student needs to replicate what the teacher does to a view which says that the student needs to successfully organise his or her own experience. In doing this, new knowledge can be constructed or at least assimilated into a previous scheme. Von Glaserfeld suggests that learning takes place when a scheme leads to a cognitive disturbance which in turn leads to what Piaget called accommodation and a re-establishment of equilibrium.

He goes on to maintain that radical constructivism does not imply a fixed way of teaching. It gives teachers the opportunity to use imaginative methods within a clear theoretical framework. He emphasises the fact that constructivism is concerned about teaching not training and as such is in direct contradiction to a behaviourist model which seems to depend exclusively on the notion of a stimulus–response mechanism as discussed earlier. He stresses the importance of language and the way in which a teacher, while he or she is not able to tell a student what concepts to construct and how to construct them, is able, by the use of a variety of linguistic utterances, to prevent the student moving in directions which experience has shown to be futile.

In essence the starting principle is that concepts are individual mental structures that cannot be passed from one mind to another. He recognises the importance of social interaction and how other minds can influence the construction but in the end the knowledge is subjective. As Von Glaserfield says:

> for the radical constructivist the crucial aspect of the negotiating procedure is that its results – the accommodated knowledge – is still a subjective construction, no matter how mutually compatible the knowledge of the negotiators may have become in the process. (p. 221)

The difficulty with this view is that identifying what real knowledge is becomes a problem. If it is different for each individual does it even cease to be a useful concept with which to explore ideas about learning? Jaworski (1994) suggests that radical constructivism does not deny the existence of an objective reality but suggests that we can never say what reality is. This again is a difficulty, as how is it possible to give meaning to something that we are unable to identify? We are then left with the idea that we are trying to develop an understanding of learning using an idea that we are unable to define in an acceptable way.

Social constructivism

This purely subjective view of knowledge and its subsequent implications for teaching were considered by Ernest (1991) in which he developed the philosophy of social constructivism. His view is that there cannot be just subjective knowledge – that there has to be objective knowledge also and that this type of knowledge is determined by its social acceptability. In elaborating on the distinction between subjective and objective knowledge he uses Popper's (1979) idea of the knowledge associated with three distinct worlds. These are the physical world, the world of our conscious experiences and the world of the logical content of books, etc. The second world is considered to be subjective knowledge and the third is objective knowledge. To this Ernest adds all intersubjective and social knowledge. This seems a helpful development of the constructivist principle. For, while it has to be true that in the end each individual will give their own meaning to knowledge that they construct, it needs to be acknowledged that the knowledge is constructed in an environment which includes social interaction with others. As Jaworski (1994) says: 'effective construal begins with fragments that can be agreed between people

... and weaves these into stories that can be discussed, negotiated and acknowledged as appropriate to a particular perspective' (p. 25).

As individuals construct their knowledge within their social environment(s), there will be the opportunity to discuss and share individual perceptions. This sharing leads to an apparent common meaning which can be construed as shared knowledge. This suggests a number of phases that the learner goes through in the construction of knowledge. These are discussed in Harlen (1992). She suggests that, initially, when learners are exposed to a new task, there is an orientation phase where pre-existing ideas are elicited. This is followed by an interaction between pre-existing ideas and new experiences and phenomena. The learner then attempts to make sense of new experiences and phenomena by constructing meaning. This is a continuous and active process which will depend on both the learning environment and the prior knowledge of the learner. During this phase the learner will restructure ideas and construct new meanings through discussion and sharing. Ideas will be clarified or exchanged. There will be conflicts to resolve as well as new ideas to construct. The ideas will then be evaluated by applying them to various situations. The final part of the cycle of learning is that of reflecting on the position reached and the changes in perception of ideas that has taken place. Thus, in constructing knowledge, students have to not only assimilate new concepts but also develop, modify and change existing ones.

These ideas were developed within a science context. It is now interesting to consider these ideas within the learning of mathematics. Ernest (1994) suggests that there are two possible forms of social constructivism: an add-on form which takes the radical constructivist view and adds to it a classroom-based social dimension and a second form which emanates from the work of Vygotsky and recognises that there are two complementary frameworks operating – Ernest calls them the intra-individual and the inter-personal. The position taken in this study is the second one. The view taken is that pupils are rational thinkers. By this is meant that pupils develop meaning within a situation in accordance with an accepted set of beliefs. These beliefs will be the pre-existing ideas which could be in the form of accepted statements. These statements will constitute the mathematical objects with which the pupil will initially interpret or give meaning to a new situation. In working in the situation the learner will either find the statements sufficient, will adapt the statements or will need to create new statements. In mathematical terms it will also be important to consider the efficiency of the statements in giving meaning to a situation. As with Harlen (1992) it will then be necessary to evaluate the knowledge constructed by reflecting on the ideas that have developed and how they relate to the starting position.

Some implications for teaching

In using these ideas on constructivism there are a number of implications for teaching. The process with which there is engagement is that of teaching, not training. This implies that the thinking processes of the pupils are more relevant than specific overt responses, and linguistic communication becomes a process for guiding a student's learning, not a process for transferring knowledge. When the learner appears to deviate from the teacher's expectations it provides an opportunity for exploring the basis on which the learner is making the perceived rational decisions. There is a tendency, particularly with low-attaining pupils, to follow an error analysis route (Rees and Barr 1984, Vanlehn 1990), in other words to assume a correct approach and to seek to ensure that the pupils become competent in this approach. However, it could be equally important to consider 'where the pupils are coming from' and what are their initial conceptions. Since these conceptions will have determined the direction in which the pupils are thinking, the role of the teacher will be to help the pupil to articulate the conception and thereby either consolidate understanding or adjust a misconception.

The links with the work of Vygotsky are now evident. It would seem reasonable to conjecture that knowledge is constructed inter-subjectively – that it is socially constructed between groups who share meanings and social perspectives of a common world. Knowledge may differ but it will be brought closer through communication. If this is true then there is a need to move from a purely individual view of knowledge to one in which the social and cultural processes of discussion and negotiation have an important role to play. The individual will construct knowledge within a social environment. Jaworski (1994) suggests that within this environment issues are raised which challenge individual construction and force changes to perceptions and thinking. In this way individual perceptions come closer together and the result is the appearance of common knowledge.

These ideas were the basis of a research project conducted by Cobb *et al.* (1995) in which they worked with second grade students. In this project with second grade pupils in the USA arithmetical computation was taught through problem-solving. The activities used were of two general types: teacher-directed whole-class activities and small group activities. Each session would end with a sharing of the ideas that had been pursued and an attempt towards developing a common understanding of what had happened in the session. Their conclusions were that an atmosphere of trust developed in the classroom and that this resulted in the pupils being enthusiastic and persistent in solving problems, and a distinct lack of frustration on the part of the pupils in the class. The role of the teacher was crucial in initiating the construction of a set of obligations and expectations. In so doing she was able to facilitate the taking of risks by the pupils in their solutions of mathematical problems.

Representation in mathematics

Finally, we briefly consider ideas related to representation in mathematics. In considering the issues related to representation and notation in developing number competence the work of Tall (1993, 1996) and Kaput (1991) is important. Tall's starting point is a consideration of why so many more children fail in mathematics than any other subject. His thesis is that the children who fail are actually carrying out a more difficult kind of mathematics than those who succeed. He found a clear tendency with low-attaining pupils to use primitive mathematical objects and primary processes, for example, counting to solve addition problems, or repeated addition to solve problems which could be more effectively solved using multiplication. In considering mathematical entities in terms of objects and processes he develops the idea of a *procept* which he defines as: 'a combined mental object consisting of a process, a concept produced by that process and a symbol that may be used to produce either.'

This idea can best be illustrated by Figure 2.1 which is concerned with number bonds and a consideration of the way in which pupils may add numbers together.

i. **Count-all** In this method the pupil would add 3 + 2 as below	ii. **Count-on** In this case 3 + 2 would be performed as:	iii. **Known fact** In this case 3 + 2 is:
* * * * * one two three one two	*** * * three four five	*** ** ***** three two five
procedure *plus* procedure	procept *plus* procedure	procept *plus* procept
leads to: * * * * * one two three four five procedure		

Figure 2.1

Tall further suggests that it is this proceptual divide that distinguishes those who progress well in mathematics and those who struggle. One reason he suggests is that those who work procedurally are always carrying out far more time-consuming work than those who can work proceptually. Thus in the study of the texts from various countries it is useful to consider how the representations and notation may be structuring pupils' thinking.

Kaput (1991) also takes the view that the way the learner understands notation and representations determines the way in which mathematical thinking can develop. He suggests that mathematical notation acts in a similar way to the architecture of a building in that it constrains and/or supports our experience. Just as Tall (1993) discusses the importance of being able to see process and concept in the same expression, Kaput talks of the importance of being able to move from something being 'form' at one level to it being 'content' at another level.

Kaput maintains that the ability to see links between different representations is a powerful problem-solving tool. He suggests that linking notational systems helps pupils to extend their reasoning processes from concrete to more abstract systems. It is also an ability clearly identified by the Russian writers (Krutetski 1976) which is present in the thinking of the able mathematical pupil.

The whole idea about how we represent concepts to pupils is also a central theme of those involved in what is called *accelerated learning* (Smith 1996). It is a challenge to all of us as teachers to find ways in which concepts can become meaningful to pupils, as when the concepts are meaningful they can be used in other contexts also. It is our belief that working mentally is an essential aspect of the whole process of finding meaning.

CHAPTER 3

Working with the whole class: developing a supportive classroom ethos

Introduction

This chapter focuses on enhancing the effectiveness of exercises in mental mathematics by discussing strategies that can be used to ensure the involvement of all the children within a supportive classroom ethos. In particular we will focus on strategies for dealing with the following potential areas of difficulty in whole-class teaching:

- The risk of children using avoidance strategies.
- The risk of children feeling 'put on the spot' in whole-class activity.
- The difficulty of achieving a pace that is suitable for all.

To begin the chapter we consider the implications of the recommendations for more direct teaching of whole classes, touching on some related issues and providing a brief review of research which has identified the benefits and drawbacks of whole-class teaching.

Whole-class teaching and the Numeracy Strategy

The Numeracy Task Force (DfEE 1998b) suggest that the recommendation that children should have regular, sustained teaching of mathematics was the most fundamental point of their preliminary report. The Task Force observed that, while the vast majority of schools gave a lot of time to mathematics, the amount of direct teaching that was received by individual children varied widely from class to class and from pupil to pupil. To confront this problem they recommend that a much higher proportion of time is spent teaching the whole class together.

Individualisation or 'over-differentiation' in mathematics teaching has been condemned as a major obstacle to effective learning. Professor David Reynolds, chairperson of the Numeracy Task Force (*Times Educational Supplement,* 10 July 1998), speaking at the launch of the Final Report of the Task Force stated that:

> We're clear about what went wrong. Methods of teaching introduced in the 70s and 80s had deleterious effects on maths in particular. All the research agrees that the one thing that badly affects performance in maths is letting children work on their own.

Implicit in these statements, or certainly the way they have been reported, is an unhelpful misconception that needs to be challenged. Galton (1998) suggests that it is common for teachers in this country to see whole-class teaching as being synonymous with didactic teaching. The suggestion, implicit in the comments of Professor Reynolds, that there was a golden age of mathematics education before the 1970s and that we should seek to return to the use of teaching methods that were employed at that time, is less than helpful in the context of the need to establish a new perception of whole-class teaching. There is no evidence to support a belief in the existence of a golden age of mathematics education and the models for whole-class interactive teaching currently being promoted owe far more to other countries than other epochs. To be fair to Professor Reynolds, he has made a number of statements on other occasions which emphasise the insertion of the word 'interactive' between 'whole-class' and 'teaching'. The emphasis on interaction helps to establish the distance between didactic teaching and the approach recommended by the Numeracy Strategy. Anita Straker, Director of the National Numeracy Strategy (NNS), provided a useful indication of the difference between past and future practice in a reply she is reported to have made to the suggestion that the NNS was recommending a return to 'chalk and talk', commenting that she was perfectly at ease with the idea as long as it was the children who were doing most of the talking and chalking.

A move to whole-class teaching

We know that the move to whole-class teaching in mathematics will represent a radical shift for many teachers. Data from the Third International Mathematics and Science Study (TIMSS) (Mullis *et al.* 1997) suggest that whole-class teaching is far less common in England than in the majority of other countries in the survey. Only 11 per cent of teachers of English Year 5 children reported using whole-class teaching regularly. Encouraging and supporting teachers in making such a shift in practice is far from unproblematic. The recommendations that came from the Leeds City Council Primary Needs Project (reported in Alexander

1997) cautioned against any authority adopting the role as arbiter of good primary practice stating that 'Good practice should henceforth be treated as problematic, rather than as an uncontentious absolute' (p. 178).

Alexander reported on the difficulty caused to some teachers in responding to the advice of the Local Educational Authority advisory team on curriculum and classroom organisation, stating that the recommendations strait-jacketed them into practice to which they had no real commitment and had difficulty managing.

Galton (1998) suggests that teachers are more likely to make decisions about when to use whole-class teaching on the basis of practical concerns rather than through considering its appropriateness for the achievement of particular learning objectives.

It is worth noting that one of the findings of the ORACLE research (see the next paragraph) was that one of the most effective groups of teachers, named the infrequent changers, made decisions about whether to work with the whole class, with groups or with individuals on the basis of the suitability of these organisational styles to different activities, particular teaching objectives and/or the nature of the children they were teaching. In the results from the standardised tests of pupil performance, the children in the classes of infrequent changers were ranked alongside the teachers who predominantly worked with the whole class. This finding resonates with the principle of 'fitness for purpose' which was promoted in the influential discussion paper on curriculum organisation and classroom practice in primary schools (Alexander *et al.* 1992).

Research into styles of teacher–pupil interaction

In this section we offer a brief summary of some of the findings of the ORACLE (Observational Research and Classroom Learning Development) Project (Galton and Simon 1980) which relate to whole-class teaching. Despite having been conducted over 20 years ago the ORACLE study remains influential, being the first observational study of its kind in the UK. For further reports of observational studies of teacher–pupil interaction see Croll and Moses (1985), Mortimore *et al.* (1987), Alexander (1991), Pollard *et al.* (1994).

The ORACLE study classified the teacher–pupil interactions that were observed into four main teaching styles. The names for three of the teaching styles (individual monitors, group instructors and class enquirers) came from the organisational strategy that dominated the practice of the teachers in each group. The fourth group were named style changers. The class enquirers interacted with the whole class for a significant proportion of the time. A higher incidence of some features of teacher behaviour that appeared to correlate with enhanced pupil performance was associated with the class enquirers. They offered the highest level of challenging questions, they were found to use praise more than other teachers and their pupils tended to learn from example as the teachers were often observed providing demonstrations. The correlation between higher order questions and whole-class interaction was confirmed by the research of Mortimore *et al.* (1987).

The ORACLE study also offered categories of pupil behaviour. In the classes of individual monitors (teachers whose interactions with pupils were predominantly with individuals) nearly 50 per cent of the children were described as intermittent workers who tended to work only when they were the focus of the teacher's attention, they 'coasted' at other times and became increasingly adept at appearing to be engaged in their work when the teacher scanned their part of the classroom. In the classes of class enquirers only 9 per cent of the children were classified as intermittent workers. The majority of the children in the classes of class enquirers, around 65 per cent, were described as solitary workers. While being more industrious, some of the characteristics of solitary workers would not fit with the vision of high quality interactive teaching that is promoted by the NNS. Solitary workers rarely contributed to class discussion and were reluctant to engage in discussion with other children.

Reference to the ORACLE research is often used to support the case for more whole-class teaching (e.g. Alexander *et al.* 1992, DfEE 1998a) and without access to the original reports of the study it is easy to gain the impression that the ORACLE findings concluded unequivocally that the whole-class approach was the most effective. In fact a sub-category within the fourth main style, the style changers, performed on a par with the class enquirers in the tests of pupil performance used within the project and achieved above average rates of interactions with individual children. The style changers were in turn sub-divided into three groups. The results of pupil performance tests suggested that the strategies used by two of the groups, the rotating changers and the habitual changers, were the least effective. The rotating changers had children moving from table to table according to the area of the curriculum they were working on. For this group the frequent disruption caused by the movement of the children led to problems of control and the loss of teaching time. The habitual changers appeared to change their organisational style in a random way and were perceived as experiencing most of the disadvantages of each organisational style and few of the benefits. The third group, the infrequent changers, altered their organisational style to suit different activities, their teaching objectives and/or the nature of the children they were teaching. In the results from the standardised tests of pupil performance the infrequent changers were ranked alongside the class enquirers as the most effective.

Avoidance strategies

Classroom observational studies have noted that whole-class teaching provides many opportunities for pupils to employ avoidance strategies. Holt (1984) described the behaviour of children he called the 'fence straddlers' who, when questions were posed to the whole class would, rather than engage in thinking of an answer, produce a mime of tortured contemplation while waiting for someone else to respond. Measor and Woods (1984) identified 'knife edgers' who again rarely engaged in thinking about a question but perfected the art of raising their hands, thus signalling their participation, but timing it so that it was unlikely that they would be asked to provide the answer. In a development of the ORACLE study Galton and Wilcocks (1983) went on to identify a sub-category of the solitary workers which they named the 'easy riders' who developed the habit of working at the slowest rate that they could get away with. The researchers noted that in mathematics it was not uncommon for as many as 80 per cent of the pupils to be engaged in easy riding.

Q2

Involvement and ethos

The increased emphasis on mental mathematics and the move to whole-class interactive teaching will make new demands on the skills and attitudes of the children. As was stated above, what separates the model for whole-class interactive teaching being promoted by the NNS from purely didactic transmission models of instruction rests in the high level of involvement of children in the talk of the classroom . We need children to offer answers and ideas, to explain their reasoning and ask questions of their teacher and classmates. The ORACLE research found that a high proportion of children did not contribute in whole-class settings. It could be argued that a reticence to take part in whole-class discussion is a function of personality and may be a characteristic of a preferred learning style that should be respected. Goulding (1992) suggests we need to beware of equating vocal participation with success in mathematics and interpreting silence as failure. If, however, we believe in the link between talk and learning, a prerequisite of effective classroom talk will be the establishment of an ethos which develops the children's confidence and leaves them free to take risks in expressing their thinking.

The importance of the task of creating a supportive classroom ethos for mathematics should not be underestimated. Research evidence suggests that experiences of learning mathematics have often had a devastating effect on peoples' attitudes towards the subject and their self-image as users of mathematics. The committee of inquiry into the teaching of mathematics in schools, which led to the report *Mathematics Counts* (1982) (usually referred to as the 'Cockcroft Report' after its chairman Dr W. H. Cockcroft), commissioned a study (Sewell 1981) of the use of mathematics by adults in daily life.

> The extent to which the need to undertake even an apparently simple and straightforward piece of mathematics could induce feelings of anxiety, helplessness, fear and even guilt in some of those interviewed was, perhaps, the most striking feature of the study. (Cockroft 1982, Para. 20)

A further indication of a widespread lack of confidence and/or distaste for mathematics came from the fact that over 50 per cent of the people who were invited to take part in the survey refused when they realised that it focused on the use of mathematics. Similar problems in finding willing participants were encountered by the Basic Skills Agency (1997) in a more recent survey.

When some of the adults involved in the study commissioned by the Cockcroft committee were questioned about their experiences as learners of mathematics, they could often identify quite specific experiences that had contributed to a deterioration of their confidence in their mathematical ability. Our own experiences of discussing attitudes towards mathematics with students and teachers have led us to identify two common negative experiences of learning mathematics which are worth considering here as they relate directly to activities which are associated with traditional approaches to mental arithmetic.

Being asked to respond at speed is identified as a source of great anxiety. The nightmare of the 'runaway test' is a common reminiscence. A victim of this experience recalls listening to question 3 in a mental arithmetic test, starting to work it out but before managing to write the answer hearing the teacher say 'question 4'. At this point they start a debate with themselves as to whether to finish question 3 or listen to question 4 only to find that debate truncated by the teacher saying 'question 5'. The other excruciating image is that of the opportunities mathematics seems to provide for public humiliation. These situations are usually related to being asked a question which under different circumstances might be fielded without difficulty but is rendered impossible by the pressure created by a mixture of the need to respond at speed and the presence of an audience that one suspects might derive more pleasure from any response other than the correct answer.

Overcoming the difficulties

In this section of the chapter we offer recommendations for strategies to overcome some of the difficulties identified above. We will stress the contribution that collaborative working can make to promoting discussion and establishing a supportive classroom ethos, and look at devices that can be used to ensure the involvement of all the children in responding to questions. The collection of activities provided with this chapter show a variety of ways in which answering devices can be used.

Working collaboratively – maths partners

Many teachers have found that it is helpful to organise children to work with a partner during mental mathematics. Talking to teachers who have experimented with this approach it is apparent that it takes time and perseverance to get the class accustomed to working in this way but it is also clear that, once established, the practice of working with a partner will offer significant benefits. Some teachers have organised the pairings by mixing abilities, with the intention of supporting the less confident children; others have avoided mixing abilities fearing that this would lead to the more confident children restricting the contribution of their partners. It would appear, however, that establishing some ground rules for working with partners based on a clear understanding of the intentions of the approach is more effective than attempts to engineer the perfect pairings on the basis of evaluations of ability and personality. The children need to be able to listen carefully to each other, to give each other the opportunity to speak and to be ready to ask questions to check and clarify understanding.

We would suggest that the most important benefits of working in pairs are the following:

- It creates a structure for the sharing of ideas and encourages mathematical talk. The quality of the exchange can also be enhanced by introducing the practice of partners reporting back to others in the class on behalf of each other. Responding to the question, 'How did your partner work out that answer?' requires good skills of listening and explanation.
- The practice of sharing an answer with a partner before sharing it with the rest of the class has two important advantages. It slows down the gap between question and response creating time for thought and allowing more children to respond. It supports the less confident children and minimises the risk of the damage to self-esteem which may result from making errors before a large audience.

Creating time for children to respond is of fundamental importance to effective interactive teaching. Rowe (e.g. 1986) conducted several studies of teacher–pupil exchanges and observed that teachers often waited no more than a second for children to respond to a question. She encouraged teachers to slow down each stage of the typical question procedure. Teachers were asked to wait just a few more seconds before asking a question, before deciding who would be chosen to provide the answer and before offering any comment on the response. The small adjustments in the pace had a number of positive effects on classroom exchanges:

- Children gave longer and more complete answers.
- The children exchanged more ideas with each other.
- It was much more uncommon to have no response to a question.
- Children expressed their ideas with greater confidence.

Answering devices

These devices are intended to reduce the opportunities for children to employ the sort of avoidance strategies that are described above. The devices would be used by individual children, although we recommend below that there should be opportunities to consult with a partner before responding, and allow the teacher to monitor the responses of all the children.

1. Digit cards

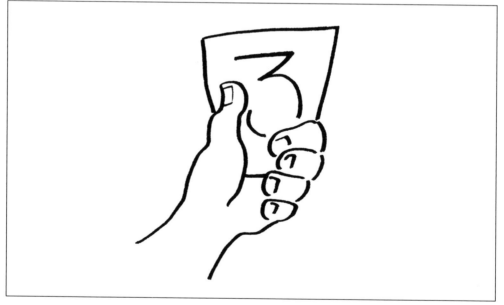

Figure 3.1

These are most suitable when children have a desk in front of them on which to lay out the cards.

2. Number petals

Figure 3.2

These lend themselves to use by children sitting on a carpet. One limitation is that the teacher needs to avoid asking questions which involve answers with numbers in which a digit is repeated. Many teachers working with older pupils have found that it is useful to add a petal that has a decimal point and an extra 0.

3. Flip overs

Figure 3.3

It could be argued that this format is more effective in supporting an understanding of place value.

4. Flashback boards

Figure 3.4

These can be purchased in the form of mini whiteboards together with the appropriate pen. A serviceable alternative can be created by laminating a piece of white card. This device can be used in other parts of the curriculum apart from number.

Using the answering devices

We would recommend the following procedure when using any of these devices.
1. The children work with their maths partner.
2. They decide on a response to a question on their own or through discussion with their partner.
3. If they have answered alone they compare their response with their partner's and can discuss any discrepancies, changing their answer if they wish.
4. At a signal from the teacher all of the children hold up their answer.

Activities using answering devices

1. Counting
Objects: Show me the number of dots on this face of the dice.
Sounds: The number of times I clap my hands (behind a book or under the desk).
Movements: The number of times I touch my head.

2. Working with specific language

- Show me the number that is *1 more than…*, *1 less than…*, *10 more than…*, etc.
- Show me an *odd* number.

- Show me a number that is *less than* 15 and *more than* 10.
- Show me a three-digit number.
- Show me *how many less than* 7 is 4? *How many more than* 5 is 8?
- Show me the *difference between* 5 and 9.
- Show me a *multiple* of 6.
- Show me a *factor* of 30.
- Show the *sum* of 7, 2 and 18.
- Show me the *product* of 6 and 7.

3. Target number
The teacher chooses a number and makes it with their number petals or writes it on their flashback board without showing the children. The children are told that the number is between, for example, 230 and 250. The children try to guess the teacher's number by selecting a number within that range and then compare it with the number selected by the teacher.

Working with the numbers points could be awarded:

For selecting a number within the range:	1 point
For selecting the exact number:	5 points
If you can say whether your number is bigger or smaller:	1 point
If you are the only person to have chosen a particular number:	2 points
If you can tell me the difference between your number and mine:	2 points.

4. Complements (pairs of numbers which add together to make a particular total)

Framework for Numeracy	Year
To 10 Show me the number you would have to add to 6 to make 10.	1
To 20	2
To 100 in multiples of 10	2
To 100 in multiples of 5 (e.g. 35 and 65)	3
To 1000 in multiples of 100	3
To 100 in all pairs of numbers (e.g. 28 and 72) (derive quickly)	4
To 1000 in multiples of 50 (e.g. 450 and 550) (derive quickly)	4
To 100 in all pairs of numbers (e.g. 28 and 72) (know)	5
To 1000 in multiples of 50 (e.g. 450 and 550) (know)	5

5. Doubles and halves
This is a version of the game 'I say... you show'. First the rule is specified – such as, you show me double the number that I say. Then the teacher says a number and the pupils have to respond by showing the number which is double the number that the teacher said. Similarly for halving.

6. Number relays

Start at 4 add on 3, take away 2, hold up the number we have arrived at.

The level of challenge can be increased by extending both the number of instructions and the range of numbers. This exercise can be differentiated by providing children with the opportunity to use a number track or a number square and follow the instructions by moving a finger to map the moves.

After some experience of the activity with a number track or square the children could be challenged to try it without the prop.

7. Function machines

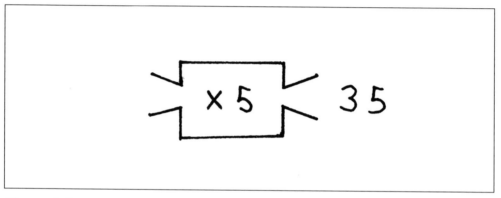

Figure 3.5

The value of this format is that children are asked to consider the input, the operation and the output or answer. The thinking involved in this exercise provides insight into the nature of the operations.

8. Guess the rule

$$
\begin{array}{ll}
1 - 3 & 1 - 3 \\
2 - 4 & 2 - 5 \\
3 - 5 & 3 - 7 \\
4 - 6 & 4 - ? \\
5 - ? &
\end{array}
$$

It will be useful to explore ideas that the children come up with as the exercise progresses. Why do you think it will be 9?

9. Odd one out

$$23, 24, 25, 29$$

Is there more than one possible answer? Explain your reasoning.

10. Addition or multiplication squares

The teacher would ask the children to show the number that they think should go into any particular square. The level of challenge of the exercise can be modified by the amount of information given in the square as shown in the examples below.

+	1	2	3	4	5
1					
2					
3					
4					
5					

Figure 3.6

x□		7			9
5		30			
	28				
				90	
8	16				
	21		3		

Figure 3.7

The use of images in the development of mathematical understanding: focusing on addition and subtraction

Introduction

The National Numeracy Strategy (NNS) provides teachers with a very detailed breakdown of the content of the mathematics curriculum which should be delivered in primary schools. Inevitably perhaps this approach can mask the 'big ideas' with which we want the pupils to engage during the different phases of their schooling. It is important however that teachers maintain a view of these big ideas and see the detail as illuminating these ideas rather than seeing the detail as leading to the big idea. Faux (1998), in exploring what these big ideas might mean in school, suggests that the big ideas for number in the primary school would be:

- Year 1 to Year 2: security in counting;
- Year 3 to Year 4: security with additive place value, and with whole numbers including chunking in groups of 3, 5, etc.;
- Year 5 to Year 6: security with multiplicative place value with whole numbers and developing a feeling for structure and structural relationships. In particular, security with multiplying and dividing by 10, 100 …

In order to explore these big ideas we need to provide pupils with images which they can use in order that they may become efficient and competent workers with number. Generally these images will be acoustic or sound images, concrete images (both visual and tactile), and symbolic images which are usually needed in order that the pupils can work numerically on paper. In thinking about the whole idea of images it is useful to consider the images that pupils most frequently experience – those used in textbooks.

Textbook images

Textbooks play an important role in influencing the ways in which teachers think about teaching and learning mathematics. It is unreasonable to expect most teachers to decide independently how to present and sequence mathematics for particular learning aims. Thus teachers inevitably use textbook schemes to help them to create images which are appropriate to the pupils with which they work. In exploring textbook images Harries and Sutherland (1999) looked at texts from a number of different countries and took the view that within a particular country textbooks reflect the dominant perspectives about what mathematics is, the mathematics which citizens need to know, and the ways in which mathematics can be taught and learnt. In other words, what appears in a mathematics textbook does not appear by chance. It is influenced by the multifaceted aspects of an educational culture. In this way mathematics textbooks provide a window onto the mathematics education world of a particular country.

Primary school mathematical concepts such as addition, subtraction, multiplication and division are all interlinked in an intimate way. For example, multiplication becomes a more powerful and efficient tool than repeated addition. But how do primary school pupils come to know about this web of interlinked concepts? The view taken was that pupils' construction of knowledge could not be separated from the external representations of that knowledge. The external representations include pictures, icons and such mathematical symbols as tables, graphs and arithmetic symbols (see also Askew 1998). They also include objects such as fingers for counting and representations which are developed for pedagogic purposes. These symbolic objects are transformative, in that they enable a person to do something which he or she could not do alone. For example, tallies on paper support an individual in counting a large number of objects; the long multiplication algorithm enables an individual to multiply together numbers which would perhaps be too large to manipulate without such a paper-based algorithm. These representations have evolved over centuries and are part of the particular culture of a country or region. Moreover, many external representations are developed (both in schools and in the world of work and training) to support learning. Pupils need to be able to see through the objects to the mathematics which underpins the representation. They need to be able to think with the representations.

The ways in which textbook writers view teaching and learning mathematics will influence how they present mathematics on a textbook page, how they sequence activities and how they structure the links between mathematical topics. Teachers have to make decisions about how to present mathematical ideas, and primary mathematics textbooks give models from which they are likely to draw.

Whereas we recognise that mathematics textbooks only represent one of the factors which influence teaching and learning, they are likely to provide valuable information on the current thinking about the learning of mathematics. This was suggested by the work of Bierhoff (1996) which compared textbooks from England, Germany and Switzerland. This study showed that German and Swiss primary mathematics textbooks:

- place a greater emphasis on mental arithmetic;
- place a greater emphasis on the wholeness of numbers rather than a place-value dissection of numbers;
- choose problems for which mathematical knowledge is a useful tool;
- place more emphasis on consolidation with more time spent on each topic and less emphasis on breadth and incorporate a very clearly defined progression of knowledge.

One of the most important results from the Bierhoff study was that Swiss and German textbooks appear to use carefully crafted problems which provoke the learning of a particular mathematical idea. In France there is also a tradition of a prior analysis of problems for particular learning aims (Brousseau 1997). In particular Brousseau's work on didactical situations has drawn attention to the fact that if learning stems from the interaction of the learner with his or her environment then the characteristics of that environment will make a difference to what is learnt. Further, our experience of teaching and learning of mathematics in Hungarian schools suggested that here also there was an emphasis on logical thinking and building connections between disparate aspects of mathematical knowledge (Harries 1997). The focus of the Bierhoff study was very much about analysing the mathematics presented in the textbooks, with an emphasis on how mathematics is transformed for learning purposes. Pupils' construction of knowledge cannot be separated from the external representations of this knowledge. Consider the representations from Hungarian and Singaporean textbooks (Figures 4.1 to 4.5). What ideas about addition and subtraction do the representations attempt to convey? Here are some possibilities – you will no doubt think of others:

- The same representation can illustrate both operations.
- One representation can generate a series of calculations.
- Representations can be static or dynamic.
- Representations can show the nature of the link between addition and subtraction – the idea of inverse.
- 'Chunking' can be used, i.e. groupings of 10 when the numbers are larger than 10, for aiding the calculation process.
- Seeing the links between the different representations helps to abstract the mathematics from the context.

Recent work of Santos-Bernard (1997) suggests that children do not necessarily read and use illustrations in the same way as authors and teachers. Drawing on the

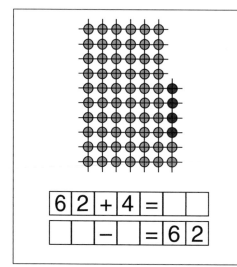

Figure 4.1

Figure 4.2

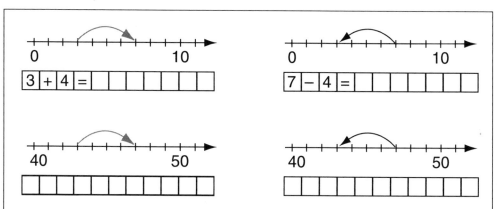

Figure 4.3

Figure 4.4

work of Campbell (1981), Duchastel and Waller (1979), Botsmanova (1972), and Shuard and Rothery (1988) she analysed the approach of pupils in both Mexico and the UK to illustrations in texts. She drew the following conclusions from her study:

- Children find it hard to extract information from two sources at once. They use mainly one of those available, and would tend to ignore the other.
- Low-attaining children tended to read the illustrations as if they represented reality rather than an approximation to it.
- Misreading of illustrative information was almost entirely located within the group of 'low-attaining pupils'.
- Whether illustrations were used or not depended very much on the nature of the question.
- It was difficult to elicit whether the pupils were to distinguish between a cosmetic and a relevant illustration. But it appeared that this was a difficulty for the low-attaining pupils.
- Pupils sometimes assume that the picture contains all the information needed for the solution of a problem rather than partial information.
- A lack of congruence between text and illustration did not appear to cause a problem, since the pupils would choose to ignore one of the representations.

She thus concluded that it was necessary for teachers and writers to recognise that there are syntactic and semantic levels of reading and interpreting illustrations and that for pupils who read the illustrations at the syntactic level confusion rather than insight was likely to result.

Images in counting and addition and subtraction

For young children the first image they use is probably not a visual one but what might be called an *acoustic image*. They listen, they hear sounds, and the rhythm of the sounds becomes meaningful. These images are developed through the use of such things as nursery rhymes through which they gain a feeling for the sound but also a feeling for the order of the sounds.

Linked with this is the idea of a *concrete image* through which the children link the acoustic image to something that is physically meaningful, such as their fingers, sets of toys. These concrete images are probably of two types – visual and tactile. Thus when they are saying or singing a rhyme they will match the sound of the numbers to a number of objects. Further they might use something like 'stepping stones' and match counting to movement.

Useful visual concrete images are such things as beads or number racks.

••••••••••0000000000••••••••••0000000000••••••••••0000000000••••••••••0000000000••••••••••0000000000

•••••00000•••••00000•••••00000•••••00000•••••00000•••••00000•••••00000•••••00000•••••00000•••••00000

Figure 4.5

Here order is the concept embedded within the image. Beads and the number rack give a sense of order through the use of colours with the beads blocked in fives or tens. Number lines, hundred squares, Gattegno charts (see Chapter 5) give a sense of order through the use of *symbols* for representing the steps along the line or the square. Here the pupils need to learn to read the symbols and relate them to the concrete and the acoustic images that they have experienced. Later they need to be able to extract the symbols from the concrete image and use it independently for the purpose of communicating aspects of number manipulation.

Reference and thinking tools

At this point we feel it is important to be clear about what these images may or may not be able to do. Let's take as an example a number line. These come essentially in two forms – the numbered number line and the empty number line. We see the numbered number line as a reference tool where everything is set out for the pupils to work with. It does not necessarily encourage flexibility but can certainly support pupils as they count in ones or tens. It tends to have a static feel to it. It is fixed and therefore leads us to view it as a reference tool. On the other hand the empty number line can be seen as a thinking tool in that before it can be used decisions need to be made – where do I put the numbers, how far apart, how will I show the jumps I make, what intermediate numbers do I need to show. This is not to say that one image is superior to the other, just that they can perform different functions. In a similar way we can consider the number square – this is usually labelled either 0 to 99 or 1 to 100. Again we would consider this to be a reference tool in that it is fixed with a set structure. If we introduce an empty number square, then we have the facility to vary the structure by changing the rule for the horizontal and vertical sequences. The focus now becomes the structure of the square rather than the numbers on it and hence the image becomes more of a thinking tool with many possibilities for exploration and investigation.

These images give the pupils tools that they can work with and think with in order to perform calculations with numbers. They provide a set of images not for the children to move through but for the children to move between as appropriate. The empty number line in particular gives the children the opportunity to work flexibly and to share information about the way in which they are thinking. Further, it links together mental work and work on paper and again it allows the children to operate between mental and written methods rather than feel that they are progressing through mental methods to written methods. What the images allow the children to do is to build up the bank of strategies from which they can choose an appropriate one for the task in which they are engaged.

Activities for counting and for addition and subtraction

The activities below are all related to the development of addition and subtraction concepts. We have tried to use activities that relate to the types of images discussed above. For pupils of all ages counting activities provide examples of acoustic images, where pupils gain a feeling for sound and the rhythm.

Counting

For young children rhymes such as the ones below can be effective.

Nine blue skittles in a row
Knock them over as you go
Nine, eight, seven …
(try varying the number and the colour).

Five little ducks went swimming one day
Over the pond and far away
One big duck said 'quack, quack, quack'
But only four little ducks came back.
Four little ducks went swimming one day
…
Three little ducks went swimming one day
…
Two little ducks went swimming one day
…
One little duck went swimming one day
…
No little ducks went swimming one day

Over the pond and far away
One lonely duck said 'quack, quack, quack'
And five little ducks came swimming back.

(Straker 1993)

Fluency with counting is an essential skill for pupils to develop from a young age as it helps to build efficiency, competence and confidence in working with number. In order to develop expertise practice is necessary. One useful way of developing this fluency is through chanting. Through the chanting the learner can hear and feel the rhythm of counting.

Depending on the year group there are many chanting activities that could be employed:

- counting forwards and backwards in ones;
- counting forwards and backwards in twos, fives, tens, starting from any single-digit number. What do we notice?
- try any starting number and any 'jump', forwards and backwards;
- try counting in one-tenths;
- try counting backwards and allow negative numbers to occur.

Some children also need to have a visual image of the counting that they are undertaking. A useful resource for this is the 'number rack'. This is easily made. It is simply a set of beads fixed on a rack as below. They are alternately 10 black and 10 white beads. You could also make one in which the beads are grouped in fives.

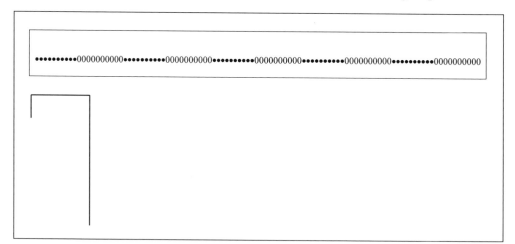

Figure 4.6

A set of bent wires like the one shown in Figure 4.6 is a useful way of speedily moving the beads in blocks of 3, 4, 5 ... The pupils can read the number off the beads since it is so clearly grouped in tens.

With and without the beads and the wire the following activities can be undertaken:

- Start at 0 and the class chant in threes or ...
- Start at 100 or another suitable number and count back in fives or ...

Further ideas

- Try counting up or down by increasing numbers (add 1, add 2, add 3 ...).
- Try the same with decreasing numbers.
- Try with decimals.

Complements

In many calculations a knowledge of complements to 10, 100 ... make the calculations both easier and quicker to perform. Chanting is a useful way of building up competence in these complements.

Teacher says and/or holds up a number and the pupils chant the complement to 10 ... The complement will be on the reverse side of the card and so the pupils start to see the complements as linked pairs. It's really a game of 'I say ...you say'.

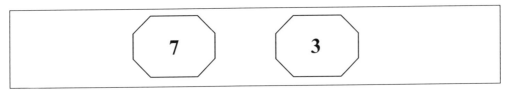

Figure 4.7

Further activities

- Try the same activity but with complements to 100, 1000.
- Try the same activity with decimals and work on complements to 1•0.

Choose an operation

Put a set of numbers on the board:

1
3
5
6
7
18
12
14
19

ADD 9

Choose an operation – in this case hold up the 'ADD 9'. The pupils have to discuss ways of adding 9 and then do the questions without showing much working.

Further activities
Try the same activity with different sets of numbers and different operations, for example, two-digit numbers and 99.
    Knowing about numbers is also an important aspect of the development of efficiency and competence. This requires a number-focused way of working rather than a process-focused way of working. In order to facilitate this we need to help the pupils to learn about the numbers.

Properties of numbers

You need two sets of cards – one with the numbers from 1 to 100 and the other with a list of properties such as square number, odd number, multiple of three … Each player has a set of six property cards and the number cards are placed face-down in a pile.

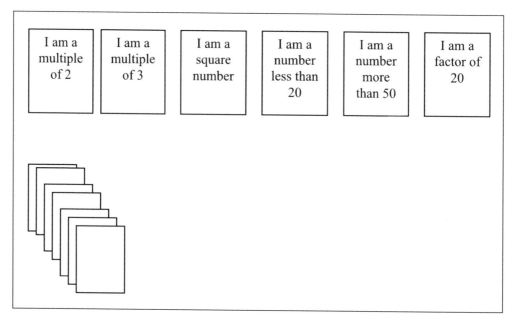

Figure 4.8

The players take it in turns to pick up a number card and check to see if it will match the property card in their hand. If it does he or she covers the property card with the number card. If not it is discarded. The first player to cover all the property cards wins.

Further activities
Now repeat the game with a new set of property cards which have two or three properties on them – for example:

I am less than 10 and multiple of 2	I am a square number less than 20

and to keep a number card it must satisfy all the properties on the card.

The same principles for images applies to addition and subtraction also:

Addition rhymes

A fat green crocodile
Eats men alive
He's eaten one already

Four will make it five.

A fat green crocodile
Eats men alive
He's eaten two already
Three more will make it five, etc.

Here comes the bus
It's going to stop
Hurry up children
In you pop.
Four inside
And six on top

How many altogether?

Further activities
Try with a variety of numbers and use cards with the number symbols on, so that the pupils see what the symbols look like

Calculation in context

Imagine a thermometer in your head. The temperature is −2°C. What is the temperature when it:

- rises by 3°C?
- falls by 6°C?
- rises by 11°C?

Further activities

- Now try a similar exercise with different temperatures.
- Try a similar exercise with distances moved.
- Try a similar exercise with money.
  (ATM 1997)

Addition/subtraction calculations using a number grid

	0	1	2	3	4	5	6	7	8	9	
	10	11	12	13	14	15	16	17	18	19	
	20	21	22	23	24	25	26	27	28	29	
	30	31	32	33	34	35	36	37	38	39	
	40	41	42	43	44	45	46	47	48	49	
	50	51	52	53	54	55	56	57	58	59	
	60	61	62	63	64	65	66	67	68	69	
	70	71	72	73	74	75	76	77	78	79	
	80	81	82	83	84	85	86	87	88	89	
	90	91	92	93	94	95	96	97	98	99	

Figure 4.9

Put the grid on an OHP or on a large chart.

First choose a sum – 'ADD 5' say. Now play the game 'I say ... you say'.

I say	you say
3	8
13	18
23	28
33	38

What do you notice? In this way we think about 'a lot for a little' – we can use what we know to perform many calculations if we realise the connections.

Now try doing 'SUBTRACT 5'. Get the pupils to describe what they are doing. What is the connection with the first activity?

The idea of inverse can be explored.

Now try the same activities with 'ADD 10' and 'SUBTRACT 10'.

Further activities

- Try the activity with different numbers. For example, how would we use the grid to add/subtract 9 or 8?
- How could we use the grid to add/subtract 23, 35 ...
- What numbers would we put in the empty cells?
- Can we extend the grid even further?

Have extra grids available with extra rows and columns on. This would allow work with negative numbers for older pupils.

A further set of activities could be based on an empty grid with rules for the way that the numbers are constructed in rows and columns – for example, that numbers go across in ones and up/down in tens.

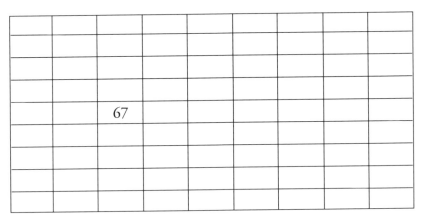

Figure 4.10

Activity 1
Put one number in the grid – say 67 (see following page). Now do counting exercises both in columns and rows.

In this way the grid becomes flexible and the range of numbers that the pupils can use within the counting exercises becomes enlarged.

Activity 2
Put one number in the grid – say 67. Now point to another cell and the pupils have to work out what number should be in the cell.

Activity 3
Change the rules on the grid – say across is in twos and up/down is in twenties. Put one number in the grid – say 67. Now do the activities above.

Using the grid (as in Figure 4.10) in this way can facilitate the development of negative numbers as an extension of the number system. Also for older pupils it could be used to work on decimals.

Activities which focus on the meaning of symbols

In all these activities the purpose is to work out what number each shade/shape represents. They are taken from a variety of Hungarian texts and are used with children from the first year in school – equivalent to Year 2 in England.

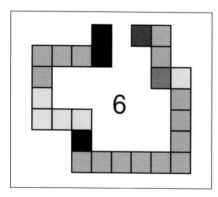

In the first network each row or column adds up to 6. Each shade of grey represents a different number (between 0 and 6). Find out what number each shade represents.

Figure 4.11

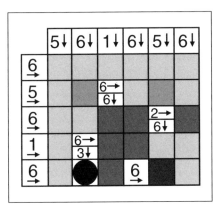

Here each shade/shape represents a different number (between 0 and 6). Each row or part-row adds up to the number indicated at the end of the row or part-row. Similarly for the columns. Find out what number each shade/shape represents.

Figure 4.12

These tasks can be given to pupils working either in pairs or in small groups. In the feedback on the activities it is important not only to check the answers but also to discuss the ways in which the pupils approached the problems and the strategies that they used in order to find out the answers.

Below are a few more challenging networks but the principle is the same. Find out what number the shade/shape represents. Once you have the principle clear then it is possible to devise numerous tasks like these for a range of different number domains.

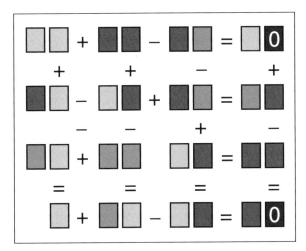

Each shade represents a different number. Find out what number each shade represents.

Figure 4.13

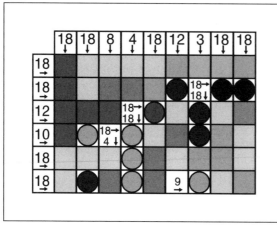

Figure 4.14

Each shade/shape represents a different number. Each row or part-row adds up to the number indicated at the end of the row or part-row. Similarly for the columns. Find out what number each shade/shape represents.

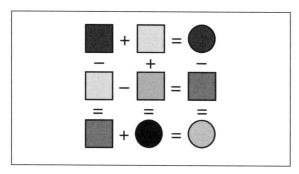

Figure 4.15

Each shade/shape represents a different number. Find out what number each shade/shape represents.

CHAPTER 5

Developing concepts of multiplication and division

Introduction

As considered in the previous chapter one of the big ideas in the later years of primary schooling is the development of security with multiplicative place value with whole numbers and developing a feeling for structure and structural relationships. So in this chapter we explore the nature of multiplication and suggest some activities which aim to help the pupils to build up firm multiplicative concepts. We have focused on the way new concepts are represented for the pupils within the topic of multiplication and division and have indicated the way in which the concepts are approached in some other countries.

In considering the issues related to the teaching and learning of multiplication and division the work of the following is particularly useful: Davydov (1991), Steffe (1994), Harel and Papert (1991), and Anghileri (1991, 1995, 1997). Normally the concepts related to multiplication are introduced through repeated addition. Using the work of Fischbein (1985), Harel and Papert (1991) suggest that under this model there are two factors.

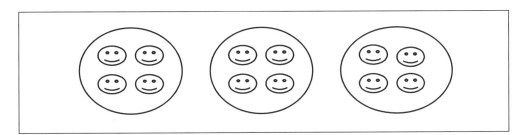

Figure 5.1

The first is the *multiplier* which is seen as the number of equivalent collections – three in the above example. The second is the *multiplicand* which is seen as the size of each collection – four in the above example. This model leads to the intuitive rules that multipliers must be whole numbers and the product must be larger than the multiplicand.

For division there are two models. One is associated with *equal sharing or partitive division* and the other is associated with *measurement* or *quotitive division*.

Figure 5.2

In the first model the whole collection is partitioned into equivalent fragments – say 24 faces into six equal groups. The size of the collection (24) is the dividend, the number of equivalent fragments (6) is the divisor, and the size of each fragment (4) is the quotient. This leads to the intuitive rules that the divisor must be a whole number, the divisor must be smaller than the dividend, and the quotient must be smaller than the dividend – i.e. division makes smaller.

In the second model – quotitive division– the idea is to find how many times a given quantity is contained in another quantity – how many groups of six faces can you make from the set above. Here there is one intuitive constraint – that divisors must be smaller than dividends.

The point to make here is not that the way we teach multiplication and division is wrong, but that as teachers we need to recognise that when these concepts are introduced, the domain of numbers that is inevitably used gives rise to certain intuitive assumptions. These assumptions can cause difficulties for pupils later as the domain of numbers that they need to use is widened.

In trying to move beyond the idea of multiplication as repeated addition, Davydov (1991) and Steffe (1994) talk about multiplication as changing the unit of calculation or developing new iterative units. Two things need to be said here. One is the need to distinguish between a model for understanding the concept of multiplication and a model for performing the calculation of a product. As a model for understanding the concept of multiplication the model of repeated addition is limited – since it does not allow for example for the ratio/proportion model to be accessed. But as a model for calculation it is necessary. Secondly, it needs to be recognised that whenever new concepts are introduced they are introduced within a context and that this context will depend on the prior experiences of the learner. Thus, when multiplication is first introduced it is inevitable that the context or number domain within which it is experienced is that of whole numbers since this relates to the learner's prior experience, and so the idea of equal groupings and repeated addition is an appropriate representation. However, what needs to be borne in mind is that when the context or number domain is extended then the concept of multiplication also needs to be revised and extended in order that it can make sense both within the old and the new context.

In order to develop this extended conceptual understanding, Anghileri (1997) considers three aspects of representation that will affect understanding – the language of multiplication and division, counting in multiplication and division, and symbolism in multiplication and division. For example, take the language of multiplication. Many different words are used: 3 times 4, 3 multiplied by 4, 3 multiply 4, 3 fours, 3 by 4, 4 threes, three lots of four. You might like to think about what these phrases mean to you and how you might represent or illustrate them for children. Some imply the idea of three groups with four in each group while others suggest four groups with three in each. Eventually children need to understand that these ideas give rise to the same answer but they can be confusing at first and could give rise to different representations or images of multiplication.

An important aspect of the early learning of multiplication is that of relating multiplication and division as inverse operations. Counting backwards and forwards in groups also helps to re-enforce the idea of multiplication and division as being inverse operations. Further, the idea of multiplication as bringing groups together, and division as splitting a whole into equal groups is useful and is strongly used in Singaporean textbooks. Resources which facilitate counting activities such as number line, stepping stones, fingers, rhythmic counting need to be used extensively especially when new concepts are introduced. As Anghileri indicates:

> Children's methods may not be the same as those taught … but frequently involve 'invented strategies' that can be fascinating to watch. It is tempting to dismiss many of these strategies as inefficient … It is true that more efficient methods will need to be developed, but fingers can provide an important link between practical and mental methods enabling abstraction to develop with understanding. (p. 47)

Symbols are important in all aspects of mathematics. They are a shorthand for representing mathematics on paper and have precise and concise meanings. Pupils need to be able read the symbols with understanding and gain an understanding of the way in which the use of the symbols facilitate the development of skills – particularly algorithmic skills.

The activities below aim to facilitate the development of the concepts outlined above recognising that:

- practical experiences prepare the children for the language of multiplication and division;
- children need to build on their own informal language;
- the interpretation of symbolic representation can be a cause of difficulty;
- there is a need to be aware of children's response to cue words in word problems and how these cue words seem to determine the operation that will be used. Anghileri (1991)

Multiplication activities

The activities suggested below are designed to help the pupils to build up their confidence and competence in both multiplication/division concepts and multiplication/division calculations. We have tried to use activities that relate to the types of images discussed in the previous chapter. For pupils of all ages counting activities provide examples of acoustic images, where pupils gain a feeling for the sound and the rhythm.

Rhymes

Ten hopping frogs
Sitting on a well
Two jumped in
And down they fell.
Eight hopping frogs
Sitting on a well
Two jumped in
And down they fell, etc.

Think about counting in groups

Further activity
Now vary the starting number and
    the number that fell in.
Fifteen little apples
Hanging from a tree
Shake the little apples
And down come three.
Twelve little apples
Hanging from a tree
Shake the little apples
And down come three, etc.

Further activity
Now start with a different number of apples and a different number falling.

Activities with beads

Make sure that you have pieces of wire of the appropriate sizes for counting in different groups.

•••••••••0000000000••••••••••0000000000•••••••••0000000000••••••••••0000000000•••••••••0000000000

Figure 5.3

Using the appropriate size wire the rack acts as a visual aid for counting in twos, threes, etc. This can be undertaken as a whole-class chanting exercise. When ten twos have been chanted the teacher can show the ways in which this can be written down:

$2 + 2 + 2 + 2 + 2 + 2 + 2 + 2 + 2 + 2 = 20$

10 lots of 2 = 20

$10 \times 2 = 20$

$10 \bullet 2 = 20$.

Counting back can be practised as a way of thinking about division as splitting into groups. So, for example, counting back from 50 in sevens shows that it can be done seven times with one left. $50 \div 7 = 7$ remainder 1, or $7 \times 7 + 1 = 50$. The pupils can do all the counting and the teacher can show on the board how what they have done can be written down using symbols.

Activities with Gattegno charts

1	2	3	4	5	6	7	8	9
10	20	30	40	50	60	70	80	90
100	200	300	400	500	600	700	800	900

This is the basic chart but of course it can be extended as below:

0.01	0.02	0.03	0.04	0.05	0.06	0.07	0.08	0.09
0.1	0.2	0.3	0.4	0.5	0.6	0.7	0.8	0.9
1	2	3	4	5	6	7	8	9
10	20	30	40	50	60	70	80	90
100	200	300	400	500	600	700	800	900
1000	2000	3000	4000	5000	6000	7000	8000	9000

This chart gives much scope for whole-class chanting activities, which can help the pupils to develop their understanding of multiplication and division concepts. They are ideal for working on multiplying and dividing by powers of 10. You will need a large chart or an OHP version of the chart which all the pupils can see.

Counting in tens

1	2	3	4	5	6	7	8	9
10	20	30	40	50	60	70	80	90
100	200	300	400	500	600	700	800	900

Activity 1
You need a pointer and a piece of string. The game is 'I point … you say'.

- Using the pointer the pupils count in ones.
- Using the pointer the pupils count in tens.
- Using the pointer the pupils count in hundreds.

In this way they connect the rhythm of counting in ones with that of counting in tens and hundreds.

Activity 2
Again the game is 'I point … you say'.

- Point to 50 and then 3 and the pupils say '53'.
- Point to 60 and then 7 and the pupils say '67'.
- Point to 200 and then 40 and then 9 and the pupils say '249'.

In doing this the pupils focus on the way in which numbers are constructed.

Activity 3
This activity focuses on counting in tens.

- Put the string on the chart so that it covers the 1 and the 20.
- Now with one end of the string fixed on the 1, move the other end of the string along the tens line and count 21, 31, 41 …

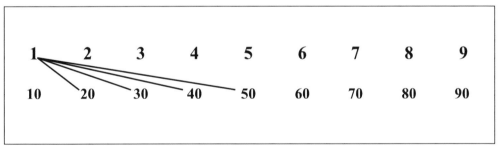

Figure 5.4

In this way the pupils see that counting in tens fixes the units digit. Repeat the exercise fixing one end of the string on any other unit digit.

Further activities

We can now repeat the exercise with the hundreds line involved also. This time the string will have two fixed points and one moves depending on whether we are counting in ones, tens, or hundreds. So we can count

- 121, 131, 141, 151 ...
- 121, 221, 321, 421 ...
- 121, 122, 123, 124 ...

For some pupils we could now use the decimal lines also and count in one-tenths or one-hundredths.

1	2	3	4	5	6	7	8	9	
10	20	30	40	50	60	70	80	90	x10 / x100
100	200	300	400	500	600	700	800	900	x10

Figure 5.5

Multiplying and dividing by powers of 10

For these activities you just need a pointer.

- First use the pointer to indicate that moving from one line to the next is 'times 10' or 'multiply by 10'.
- Get the pupils to say this as you move the pointer from the units row to the tens row.
- Now point to a number, say 6 – the pupils say '6'.
- Move the pointer to the next row – the pupils say 'times by 10' or 'multiply by 10'.
- Stop at the 60 – the pupils say 'equals 60'.

You can repeat the exercise but now using the tens and the hundreds rows. You can now use the units and the hundreds rows to repeat the exercise for multiplying by 100.

For division the process is repeated but working in the opposite direction (see Figure 5.6).

Further activities

The exercises can now be extended using some extra rows. This would allow the pupils to work with decimal numbers, and to think about multiplying and dividing by 0.1, 0.01 ...

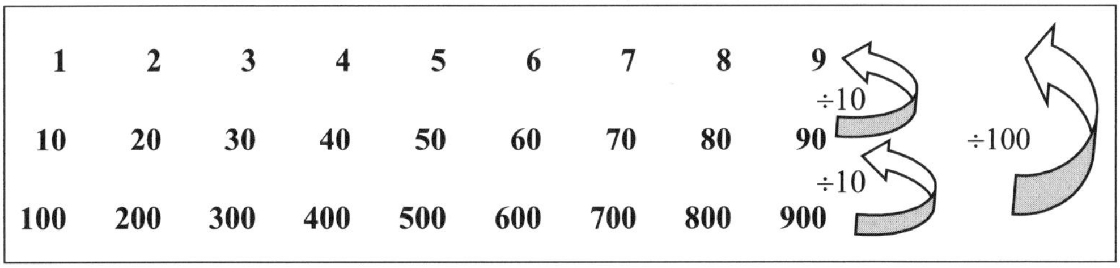

Figure 5.6

Multiplying and dividing by ten for two-digit numbers

The number lines should be either on a large chart or on an OHP. You will need a pointer or a piece of string. Again it is the 'I point … you say' game.

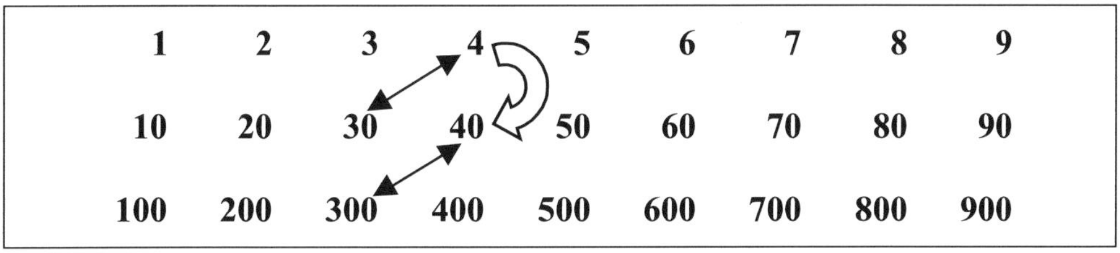

Figure 5.7

- Place the pointer across 30 and 4 – the pupils say '34'.
- Move the pointer to the next row – the pupils say 'times by 10'.
- Hold the pointer over the 300 and 40 – the pupils say 'equals 340'.

For division we reverse the movement.

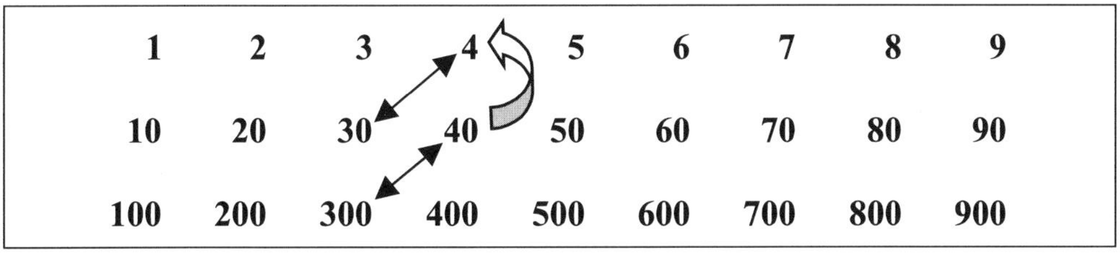

Figure 5.8

- Hold the pointer over the 300 and 40 – the pupils say '340'.
- Move the pointer to the next row – the pupils say 'divided by 10'.
- Place the pointer across 30 and 4 – the pupils say 'equals 34'.

Further activity
Extend the number domain to include decimals. Write the sum on the board as the pupils say it so that they can relate the symbols to the chanting.

Using grids

	2	3	4	5	6	7	8	9	10	11
0	0	0	0	0	0	0	0	0	0	0
1	2	3	4	5	6	7	8	9	10	11
2	4	6	8	10	12	14	16	18	20	22
3	6	9	12	15	18	21	24	27	30	33
4	8	12	16	20	24	28	32	36	40	44
5	10	15	20	25	30	35	40	45	50	55
6	12	18	24	30	36	42	48	54	60	66
7	14	21	28	35	42	49	56	63	70	77
8	16	24	32	40	48	56	64	72	80	88
9	18	27	36	45	54	63	72	81	90	99
10	20	30	40	50	60	70	80	90	100	110
11	22	33	44	55	66	77	88	99	110	121
12	24	36	48	60	72	84	96	108	120	132

Figure 5.9

As the pupils learn more and more tables it is useful to keep a record as in the chart above by adding to the columns as time goes by. It is also useful to use the chart as an aid to the learning of the tables.

	2	3	4	5	6	7	8	9	10	11
0					0					
1					6					
2					12					
3					18					
4					24					
5					30					
6					36					
7					42					
8					48					
9					54					
10					60					
11					66					
12					72					

Figure 5.10

Using the grid as above the pupils can chant through the table and gain a feeling for the sound of the table.

Next remove some of the numbers from the table as below:

	2	3	4	5	6	7	8	9	10	11
0					0					
1					6					
2										
3					18					
4										
5										
6					36					
7					42					
8										
9					54					
10										
11					66					
12					72					

Figure 5.11

- Now the pupils do the chanting with some of the numbers missing. Again they gain a feeling for the sound of the table but do not always have the visual aid.
- Now remove all the numbers from the table except 6, 36 and 72 and repeat the exercise.
- This can be repeated with other tables as they become known and also with groups of tables.

Multiplication tables (from MT163)

This is an activity for helping the pupils to learn their tables (see over page). For a particular table – in this case times 6 – the teacher points to a number on the outside of the spider and the pupils together reply with the number of sixes in that number.

Further activity
Make a set of spiders (see Figure 5.12) for each table and use as appropriate to practise the particular table.

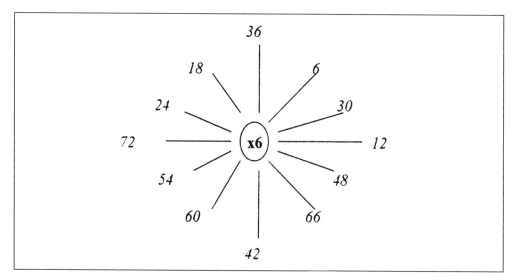

Figure 5.12

Activities which focus on the use of interpretation of symbols

All these activities focus on multiplication and division.

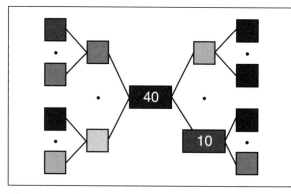

Figure 5.13

The target number for the given grid of numbers is above the grid. We want to achieve the target number by multiplication. Place the given shape over a set of numbers on the grid so that the numbers multiply to give the target number.

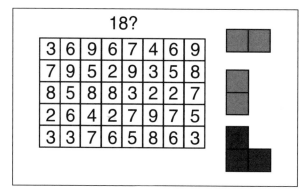

Figure 5.14

Each shade in the network represents a different number. Each pair of numbers one at end of a branch multiply to give the number on the other end. Find out what number each shade represents.

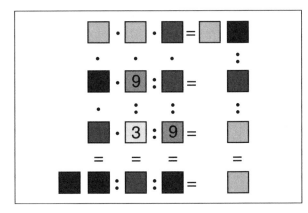

Figure 5.15

Each shade in the network represents a different number. The operations involved are multiplication and division and all the sums vertically and horizontally must be correct. Find out what number each shade represents.

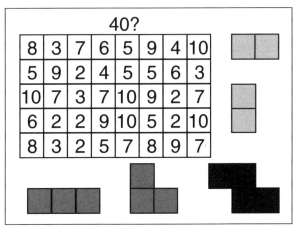

Figure 5.16

The target number for the given grid of numbers is above the grid. We want to achieve the target number by multiplication. Place the given shape over a set of numbers on the grid so that the numbers multiply to give the target number.

Each shade in the network represents a different number. Each group of four numbers multiply to give the number in the centre of the group. Find out what number each shade represents.

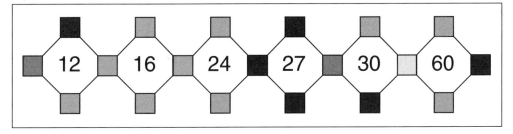

Figure 5.17

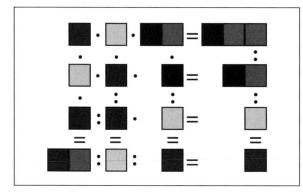

Each shade in the network represents a different number. The operations involved are multiplication and division and all the sums vertically and horizontally must be correct. Find out what number each shade represents.

Figure 5.18

These tasks can be given to pupils working either in pairs or in small groups. In the feedback on the activities it is important not only to check the answers but also to discuss the ways in which the pupils approached the problems and the strategies that they used in order to find out the answers. Once you have the principle clear then it is possible to devise numerous tasks like these for a range of different number domains.

CHAPTER 6

Using and applying mental mathematics

Introduction

This chapter focuses on the use and application of knowledge and skills within the context of mental mathematics. We will consider the relationship between the National Curriculum and the National Numeracy Strategy (NNS).

The development of educational policy and practice in this country is often characterised by 'pendulum change' in which we abandon one set of established principles for another, often without any meaningful debate. Pendulum change often results in babies being thrown out with the bath water.

With the introduction of the NNS it would seem to be a worthwhile exercise to examine which aspects of the National Curriculum, prior to the latest revision (DfEE 1999b), are being taken forward and which, if any, are being abandoned. In particular we will focus on the place of the use and application of mathematics within the NNS. We will suggest that this aspect continues to be of paramount importance and provide examples of how the structure of the daily mathematics lesson lends itself to involving children in investigative work. The chapter ends with suggestions for activities which will engage children in developing the skills of use and application within mental activity.

The new agenda

The NNS has brought new priorities to the teaching of mathematics. A useful summary of the key messages of the NNS has been provided within the training materials for leading mathematics teachers (DfEE 1999c):

- emphasis on mental calculation
- delay (in the teaching of) written methods
- teaching of mental strategies
- manageable differentiation
- direct teaching of the whole class
- interactive teaching
- variety of teacher presentation.

The content of the draft version of the New National Curriculum for Mathematics (DfEE 1999b) and the Framework for Numeracy (DfEE 1999a) correspond exactly. The main differences between these two documents and previous versions of the National Curriculum are ones of emphasis rather than content. Some differences in emphasis can be detected by comparing the definition of numeracy offered by the NNS with that from other sources. The Cockroft Report (1982) felt that numeracy was proved by use in the real world. To be considered numerate the report suggests that we would need 'an ability to make use of the mathematical skills which enables an individual to cope with the practical demands of his everyday life' (para. 39), coupled with an ability to understand information presented in mathematical form. Nunes and Bryant (1996) suggest that 'being numerate involves thinking mathematically about situations' (p. 19). They state that to be numerate it is not enough to learn mathematical procedures; the procedures need to be translated into thinking tools that can be related to situations in which they serve a purpose. The NNS (DfEE 1999a) definition of numeracy appears to be located within the context of the school rather than daily life. Numerate pupils will be 'confident enough to tackle mathematical problems without going immediately to teachers or friends for help' (Section 1, p. 4).

The main success criteria for the Numeracy Strategy has been established as being 75 per cent of children achieving Level 4 or above in the Key Stage 2 National Tests by 2002. We are not suggesting that success in standardised tests and the creation of numerate adults are mutually exclusive aims but there is evidence to suggest that we cannot assume that success in tests automatically translates into a level of numeracy that is functional in everyday life.

The use and application of mathematics

It could be argued that the inclusion of an attainment target that focused on the use and application of mathematics was one of the most significant contributions the National Curriculum has made to mathematics education. By placing use and application within a statutory framework the development of the skills of mathematical thought and enquiry became an entitlement for all children. The *Non-statutory Guidance* (NCC 1989) stated that 'using and applying mathematics ... should stretch across and permeate all other work in mathematics, providing both the means to, and rationale for, the progressive development of knowledge, skills and understanding' (p. D3).

The application of mathematical skills and knowledge was also one of the key themes of the Cockroft Report *Mathematics Counts* (1982). This report remains the most comprehensive review of the teaching of mathematics in this country and was intended to shape mathematics education for the remainder of the twentieth century. The Report suggested that problem solving, which it defined as 'the ability to apply mathematics to a variety of situations' (para. 249), needed to be at the heart of the subject. Teaching approaches that provided opportunities for discussion, practical work and the application of skills in meaningful contexts were recommended as the essential ingredients of a diet which could produce confident and capable mathematicians.

The recommendations of the report were based on wide-ranging research including enquiries into how adults used mathematics in everyday life (see Chapter 3) but many of the messages were not new. The methods used to teach mathematics have been questioned consistently over a long time. McIntosh (1977) provides a useful historical survey of written comment on mathematics education. Three extracts from the survey are reproduced below.

> If a child be requested to divide a number of apples between a certain number of persons, he will contrive a way to do it ... They should be allowed to pursue their own method first ... When pupils learn through abstract examples, it very seldom happens that he understands a practical example the better for it ...' (*Intellectual Arithmetic*, p. IV, 1840, quoted in Floyd 1981, p. 9)

> When children obtain answers to sums and problems by mere mechanical routine, without knowing why they use the rule ... they cannot be said to have been well versed in arithmetic. (*Reports*, 1895, in Floyd 1981, p. 9)

> Instruction in many primary schools continues to bewilder children because it outruns their experience. Even in infant schools, where innovation has gone furthest, time is wasted in teaching written 'sums' before children are able to understand what they are doing. (The Plowden Report *Children and their Primary Schools* 1967, p. 196, in Floyd 1981, p. 8)

These extracts suggest a longstanding disjunction between the mathematics that is taught and that which can be used and applied by the learner. The following passage, taken from a more recent official review of mathematics education, suggests that there is little reason to believe that the problem has been overcome.

It is important to note that most pupils can perform the basic skills adequately if they know which operation (e.g. addition, subtraction, multiplication or division) is required. They can usually do the calculation. Problems arise when the question is in a context and the individual pupil has to decide which mathematical operation to use. (OFSTED 1993, p. 20)

The attainment target on the use and application of the National Curriculum was a response to this apparent lesson of history that, when mathematics is presented as a collection of techniques and routines to be rehearsed and facts to be committed to memory, it seldom results in the acquisition of skills or knowledge that can be applied. The working party that composed the programmes of study for the use and application of mathematics set out to describe the skills that characterise and facilitate mathematical thought and enquiry. The majority of these skills are now found listed in the solving problems section of the teaching objectives of the *Framework for Teaching Mathematics* (DfEE 1999a).

Opinions as to the importance of the investigative approaches that are associated with the use and application of mathematics will be influenced by the view held by each individual as to the purpose of the subject. Ernest (in Nickson and Lerman (eds) 1992) identifies three philosophies of mathematics education: absolutist, viewing the subject as a body of fixed, irrefutable knowledge; progressive absolutist, which shares the absolute view of mathematical knowledge but attributes a role to the individual in extending that knowledge; and social constructivist, which sees mathematical knowledge as the fallible and ever-changing product of human creative activity. Many would argue that the absolutist philosophy which manifests itself in education in utilitarian aims for the subject and a rigid emphasis on the practice of basic skills has remained the predominant influence over school mathematics.

A more expansive and descriptive view of the purpose of mathematics education has been offered by Papert (1972) who suggests that we should be teaching children to be mathematicians rather than merely teaching them something about mathematics. He observed that the traditional school experience of the subject could be distinguished from the activity of a mathematician by the fact that the mathematician is involved creatively in the 'pursuit of a personally meaningful project'.

If we accept that genuine mathematical activity is characterised by creativity, children need to be encouraged to explore aspects of the subject and make their own discoveries. Bruce (1991) suggests that the skills developed through engaging children in problem-solving and investigational activities have a far wider significance, stating that these skills contribute to 'a sense of control over our lives', which in turn engenders 'self-esteem, self-confidence, autonomy, intrinsic motivation, the desire to have a go and take risks, to make decisions and to choose' (pp. 81–2).

A belief in the fundamental importance of having a section of the statutory curriculum explicitly devoted to use and application has led the mathematics education representatives in successive National Curriculum working parties (1987, 1992, 1994) to fight for its continued existence as a separate entity (Spooner, in Coulby and Ward 1996). The revised National Curriculum (DfEE 1999c) does not include a separate section of the programmes of study for use and application. Instead this element is a specified part of each of the other sections.

It should be noted that the interpretation of the attainment target for use and application has proved difficult for teachers (Millett and Askew 1994). There has also been criticism of the apparent lack of analysis of the links between problems that are set for children in this country and the mathematics they will need to use in solving them (see Chapter 4). If there is a suspicion that a less prominent place within the statutory curriculum for an aspect of mathematics that has proved difficult for many teachers to implement will detract from the emphasis given to the application of mathematical knowledge and skills, it could be counteracted by many of the prominent elements of the approach recommended by the NNS. Attainment Target 1, Using and Applying Mathematics (NCC 1989), contained three major themes: using mathematics, communicating in mathematics and developing ideas of argument and proof.

A key objective for the NNS is that children should build an extensive repertoire of mental calculation strategies from which they can select an approach which suits the numbers they are working with. The principle of selecting approaches to calculation could be highly significant in improving individuals' confidence in using mathematics in general. The ACACE (Advisory Council for Adult and Continuing Education) research (Sewell 1981, in Cockroft 1982) discovered a group of adults who although capable of performing most calculations that were required of them 'felt a sense of inadequacy because they were aware that they did not use what they considered to be the proper method' (para. 22).

The structure of the three-phase lesson should also provide many opportunities to communicate mathematical ideas. Children will learn to appreciate that there is an audience for their ideas and the methods they employ and this in turn will develop their metacognitive awareness.

The section of the teaching programmes of the *Framework for Numeracy* entitled 'reasoning about numbers or shapes' contains most of the essential elements of the argument and proof section of Attainment Target 1. Direct, interactive teaching of approaches to investigation, problem-solving, making generalisations, predicting and extending enquiry should enable children to develop these key mathematical skills through the discussion and comparison of a range of approaches.

Independent group work within the daily mathematics lesson

Amongst the fundamental principles of the teaching approach recommended by the NNS is the idea that the whole class should be working within the same mathematical theme and that differentiation should be limited. The NNS recommends that when teachers work with groups within the second phase of the three-phase lesson they should try to organise children into no more than four groups covering three levels of ability. An intention of this arrangement is to provide time for the teacher to engage in direct teaching with one group, and for this to happen the other three groups need to be engaged in an activity which they can carry out independently. The challenge of selecting and preparing activities that are both meaningful and capable of being carried out without the support of the teacher is immense.

In the remainder of this chapter we will suggest that there are two valuable models for activities which are both productive and able to be carried out independently. The activities are intended to engage children in an investigative approach in that they will be placed in situations where they need to select the mathematical knowledge and skills that will need to be applied. The first group of activities are based around responses to 'open' questions, i.e. questions for which there are a number of different answers. Fisher (1995) suggests that while there is a place for closed questions the 'search for the "quick-fix" of a single correct answer' is a major obstacle to thinking.

The major benefits of open mathematical questions might be summarised as follows.

- The exercise of responding to an open question encourages children to review and retrieve knowledge that is relevant to the question posed. The act of selecting mathematical knowledge and concepts that are relevant to a particular situation is one of the fundamental principles of the use and application of mathematics. When we involve children in this type of activity they enhance the sense of 'ownership' of aspects of their mathematical knowledge. Knowledge that has been selected and applied is more likely to be used again.
- In terms of assessment it could be argued that knowledge demonstrated in response to open questions provides a more reliable indication of understanding.
- This type of exercise also gives children the opportunity to surprise us by exceeding our expectations. If we ask the question '2 × 8' and get the answer '16' we know that a child, at this point in time, can recall this particular number fact (or has a strategy for calculating it). If we say that the answer to a mathematical question is 16 and ask what the question could have been and receive the following responses:

- $20 - 4$
- $2 + 8 + 6$
- 4×4
- $32 \div 2$
- $64 \div 4$
- 4^2

we learn that children have a range of other number facts. Arguably of greater importance is that the exercise gives the opportunity to explore the relationship between the number operations.

- The activities are differentiated by outcome, providing greater challenge for some pupils without excluding others.

Organisation

This is an approach that will need plenty of practice. Atkinson (1991), who provides many excellent examples of children working on 'open' tasks, cautions that when starting out with this approach we can expect the children's insecurity to show itself. By working together as a class initially to provide models of what is expected we can expect them to adapt successfully to this way of working.

The approach can be used within the 'warm-up' phase of the lesson in the following way:

- After setting the question the children would work with their maths partner (see Chapter 3) for a short period of time. We would recommend one to two minutes for the youngest children or when the activity is new to the class, extending to five minutes (when the question is appropriate) for older children and children who are used to working in this way.
- The children discuss an open question and collect together ideas which can later be shared with the rest of the class. A list of vocabulary might be provided as a prompt.

Figure 6.1

In some cases the question could be left 'open' for a set period of time (a week or two) with the ideas collected in the first feedback session displayed and then added to as time progresses ending in a final sharing and review session.

An example:

What patterns can you see in this grid?

1	2	3
4	5	6
7	8	9

Figure 6.2

Possible responses:

- The rows add up to 6, 15 and 24 (there is a difference of 9).
- The columns add up to 12, 15 and 18 (there is a difference of 3).
- The diagonally opposite numbers in the corners add up to 10.
- The number in the centre of each row is one third of the total of the row.
- The number in the centre of each column is half the sum of the numbers at the top and bottom of each column.

Extending

If the activity is to be extended over a longer period, when the observations that the children have made are collected, it will also be useful to encourage them to pose questions as to how they might continue to explore the relationships seen within the grid. If the children are not used to posing questions in this way some examples can be given. For example:

- What happens if instead of starting with 1 as the first number we start at 10?
- What happens if we enter consecutive even or consecutive odd numbers?
- What would happen in a grid that was 4 by 4?
- What would happen if the grid was 4 by 3?

Questions would become part of the display and then explored by the children during the rest of the time set aside for working on the theme.

This type of activity can also make a valuable contribution to the management of the daily mathematics lesson. When the main teaching activity is conducted the groups working independently will need to know what they can do when set exercises are completed. The 'open question' exercises can be established as 'ongoing contingency activities', i.e. something that children return to when they have time in their daily mathematics lessons. The starting points might also be used as a focus for a homework task.

Further examples

1. Treasure boxes (see Figure 6.3)
Tell me everything you can about what is inside your box.

Treasure boxes are filled with collections of small objects. It is useful to put the objects in groups of different numbers, e.g. six buttons, four counters, two conkers, etc. The children empty their box and then report on the contents. It will be helpful to provide some keywords that children might use.

They might report:

- how many in each set of objects
- comparing the sets … there are more, less … than …
- the largest/smallest set.

Figure 6.3

2. What numbers can you make with the digits 4, 3, and 7 and the operations +, −, and ×?
You must use all three digits only once for each new number, for example:
    $7 + 4 + 3 = 14$ $43 − 7 = 36$

3. What is the same and what is different about these two shapes and these two numbers?

Square   Rhombus (of same dimensions)

   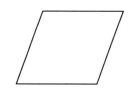

Responses might include:

Same
The sides all the same length
Four sides
Diagonally opposite angles
are equal
Two pairs of parallel sides
They are both 2-D shapes
They are both quadrilaterals.

Different
The square has four right angles
The rhombus has two obtuse and two
acute interior angles

4. The answer is 16, what could the question be?

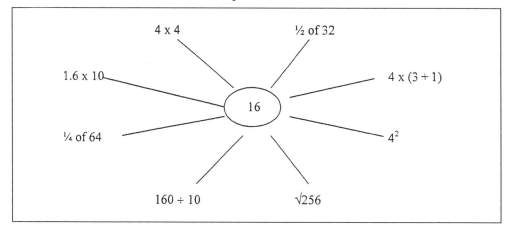

Figure 6.4

5. Where have you seen right angles, circles, triangles, parallel lines, etc.?
6. Make up stories for these number sentences:
    $3 + 7 = 10$, $8 − 4 = 4$, $2 × 4 = 8$ etc.

or a story to describe this sequence of number sentences:
50 – 36 = 14 ... 14 – 6 = 8 ... 8 + 50 = 58 ... 58 ÷ 2 = 29

7. Make different shopping lists of things that could be bought if you had £2.

Figure 6.5

8. Tell me everything you can about these numbers, these shapes, this graph
   or give some examples of:
   Doubles, halves, big numbers, multiples of 9, special numbers, number
patterns, 2-D shapes, quadrilaterals, things that are heavier than 1 kilogram, etc.

Figure 6.6

9. Find ten (or as many as you can)

- numbers that are larger than 5 but less than 20
- odd numbers less than 25
- odd numbers that are less than 50 but more than 30
- multiples of 4
- multiples of 4 which end with 4
- numbers and their doubles

- numbers that can be made with the digits 1, 2, 3 and 4
- words that can be used to describe the position of an object
- pairs of numbers with a difference of 5
- odd numbers that are multiples of 3
- sets of three consecutive numbers which have an odd total
- amounts that can be made exactly using just 2p and 5p coins
- 2-D shapes that have at least one pair of parallel sides
- square numbers.

10. Make different mathematically correct sentences using these words and
   numbers:
Consecutive, odd, even, multiple, factor, square number, rectangular number,
prime number
   7, 12, 21, 23, 25, 27, 24
   (vocabulary selected from National Centre for Literacy and Numeracy (1999d)).

Mathematical games

The second group of activities are mathematical games. We would recommend
that the games are introduced to the whole class by playing together as a whole
class and then the games can become part of a collection that can be played by
pairs or groups of children either as part of a planned activity or as a contingency.

Before providing a small selection of games we offer a brief summary of some
guidance on the use of mathematical games which was created by a working party
of teachers.

Purposes and advantages of using maths games:

- They provide the opportunity to practise and reinforce newly acquired skills.
- They increase speed and accuracy in the use of skills.
- They present skills in a different context.
- They allow non-tedious reinforcement.
- They encourage enthusiasm for maths.
- Used as homework activities they can encourage parents to readdress
  stereotypical attitudes towards mathematics.
- They can help bridge the gap between practical activities and more abstract
  ideas or methods of recording.
- They present maths in a relaxed atmosphere.
- They provide opportunities to use and extend mathematical language.
- They promote cooperation.

Negative aspects which need to be controlled and monitored include:

- the effects of the game becoming over-competitive;
- the possibility of repeated failure – games in which success depends on both an element of luck and skill provide more equal opportunities for success and make failure easier to rationalise;
- the tendency to ignore the need for progression – the mathematical content of any game needs to be analysed and the best games will allow play at a variety of levels.

Using games effectively

It was noted that the introduction of maths games often required a great deal of teacher time and that many games only achieved their full potential if an adult could be present when they were played.

To overcome these problems the following strategies have been suggested:

- Focus on a limited number of high quality games.
- Formats for games that can be re-used at different levels through the school will be useful.
- Use adult classroom support for maths games.
- Use review/carpet time to introduce game to whole group.
- Use cascade method where children who know the game teach others.
- Use older children to play/oversee younger children.
- Try to build a routine of maths games going home. Making sure that rules and purposes are made clear to parents.
- Identify learning outcomes for games and relate them to teaching programmes through schemes of work.
- Involve the children in establishing ground rules for game playing.
- Analyse the learning that we can expect to come from a game so that we justify time spent on playing it to anyone who might question the relevance of the activity.
- Encourage older children to prepare/invent games for younger ones.
- Look for games that offer the correct balance between chance (so everyone can win sometimes) and skill (providing a context for use and application and the possibility of improving strategy, etc.).

Some ideas to try:

- game of the week
- evaluation of games from children
- use playtime games and playground games

- introduce games from other cultures
- family history: games we used to play.

Some games to try

Spotty Snake

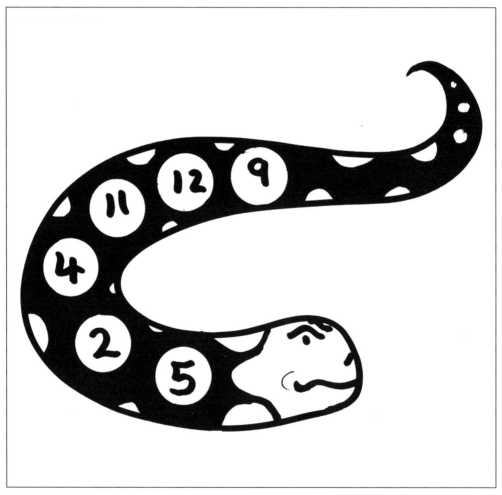

Figure 6.7

- This is a game for two people each with their own snake, two dice and eleven counters each.
- Take turns to roll the dice.
- Add the scores together.
- If you can, cover the number scored with a counter.
- The winner is the one to cover all the numbers.

Doubles

- Play with a partner and each draw a grid like the ones below.
- Take turns to roll the dice.
- Double the number rolled.
- Write the answer in any box on your grid.
- Carry on until each grid is full.
- Now take it in turns to roll the dice again.
- If you can, cross out the double of the number thrown.
- The winner is the first person to cross out all of the numbers.

Figure 6.8

Stingo

- Play with a partner and two dice.
- The objective is to claim as many of the numbers on the 1 to 12 grid as possible.
- Throwing the two dice, numbers can be claimed by using either the sum or the difference of the numbers thrown to make one of the numbers on the playing grid, for example, throwing 2 and 5 could either score 7 (2 + 5) or 3 (5 − 2).
- If the only numbers you can make are taken you miss a turn.

1	2	3
4	5	6
7	8	9
10	11	12

Figure 6.9

Flags

Play with a partner and three dice. The objective is to claim four connecting numbers, i.e. four numbers which are either vertically or horizontally adjacent (see Figure 6.10). Numbers can be claimed by:

- throwing the three dice
- using the scores thrown in any of the following ways (or any other way which is mathematically correct) to make one of numbers on the playing grid, for example, a throw of 2, 3, 5.

$2 + 3 + 5 = 10$ $23 + 5 = 28$
$5 + 3 - 2 = 6$ $35 - 2 = 33$
$5 \times 3 \ 2 = 17$ $2^3 + 5 = 13$

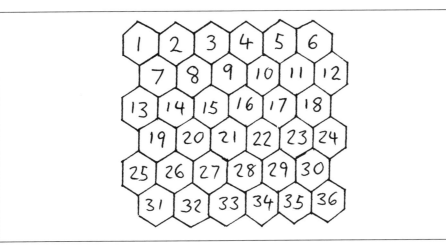

Figure 6.10

Risky Business

- Two, three or four people can play with two dice.
- Each player needs a pencil and paper.
- Each player start with 0.
- Take it in turns to roll two dice as many times as you like.
- Each time either add or multiply the two numbers you roll.

NB. You must decide whether to add or multiply the dice scores before you start and stay with your choice throughout the game.

- Add the sums or the products to your previous total and write it on your paper.
- Choose when to end your turn.
- You can choose a target total before you start (e.g. 100 when adding the scores or 250 when multiplying) or you can agree to see who is ahead after a certain number of goes (e.g. 10).

Beware! If you roll a 5 you lose your score for that go. If you roll a double 5 you lose all of your score!

Crossing the River

The objective of the game is to get all your counters across the river. This is a game for two players with two dice. Each player has twelve counters that they put on his or her bank of the river against any of the numbers. Any number of counters can be put on each of the numbers (see example in Figure 6.11). The players take it in turns to throw two dice. The sum of the two dice scores shows the position from which one counter may cross the river. The player who gets all his or her counters across first is the winner.

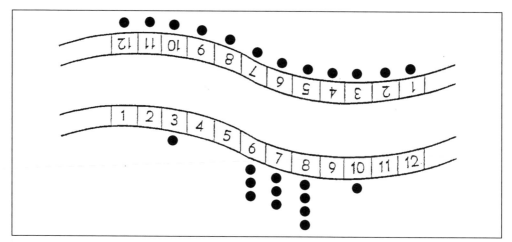

Figure 6.11

Success in this game is governed by the probability of throwing certain scores, for example, 7 – there is a higher probability (6:36) of throwing 7 as it can be made by 6 and 1, 1 and 6, 2 and 5, 5 and 2, 3 and 4 and 4 and 3, whereas 2 can only be made by throwing a double 1.

After the children have played the game a few times you might wish to encourage the children to think about where to place the counters and investigate the different possible combinations for each score.

Card Games

Two card games working on number bonds to 10:

Rummy

- Put several sets of 1 – 9 cards together.
- Deal out four cards to each player.
- Put the rest in a pile with the top card placed face-up to start another pile.
- Players put down any pairs they have that add up to 10, then continue trying to make new tens by choosing cards from either pile (i.e. the top card in the pile which is face-up or from the pile which is face-down) to replace cards that have been placed in pairs.
- The players must always have at least four cards (until the game finishes) but may have several more.
- At each turn a player can both make a pair and take new cards or pick up a new card. You cannot pick up cards first and make pairs in the same go.

Snap

- Players each have half a pack made up of several suits of 1 – 9 cards.
- Play as normal snap except by calling 'snap' when two cards add up to 10.

Playing card challenge

- This activity needs three children working together performing three different roles: a dealer, a player and referee/timekeeper (if an adult is involved they can be both dealer and referee).
- Use a complete pack of cards with the face cards removed (i.e. Ace to 10).
- The dealer turns over the top two cards.
- The player must give the product, the sum or the difference of the value of the two cards shown. (NB: Before the game begins it is agreed which operation [+, −, ×] is to be used.)
- The referee/timekeeper stops a clock to check the answer given (perhaps with a calculator).
- The player keeps cards that received a correct answer.
- The referee/timekeeper starts the clock again when the next two cards are turned over.
- By playing against the clock the children have an idea of a record time (for the whole pack or cards collected in 60 seconds) and they can try to improve their record over time.

Twist or Stick

- This activity needs two children working together taking turns to be the dealer and the player.
- Use a complete pack of cards with the face cards removed (i.e. Ace to 10).
- The object of the game is to get as many of the 40 cards as possible.
- The dealer turns over the top two cards.
- The player gives the product of the value of the two cards.
- If the player gives the correct product they keep the cards.
- On the first go if the player gives the wrong product they have one more go.
- If they are wrong the second time they switch roles and become the dealer.
- The player can then choose to twist (ask for two more cards) or stick with the cards they have won.
- If they choose to twist, before the next two cards are turned over they must say whether they think the product of the new cards will be greater or smaller than the product of the previous two cards.
- If they give the correct product and have guessed the relative size of the products correctly they keep the cards and can decide whether or not to play again.
- If they give the product incorrectly or have guessed the relative size incorrectly the cards are returned to the pack and they become the dealer.

CHAPTER 7

Supporting activities

Introduction

In this chapter we provide further models for activities to extend the variety offered in the previous chapters. In Chapter 1 we made a case for the need for variety in a programme of mental mathematics on the basis of maintaining the interest and motivation of the pupils, developing active and purposeful learning and the need to work on specific skills. Some teachers have found it helpful to timetable different activities for specific days over a two-week period, e.g.:

	WARM-UP ACTIVITY
MONDAY	**Number fan activities**
TUESDAY	**Follow-me game**
WEDNESDAY	**Listening activity**
THURSDAY	**Counting activities**
FRIDAY	**Open questions/discussion activity**
MONDAY	**Elimination games**
TUESDAY	**Memory activity**
WEDNESDAY	**Estimation activity**
THURSDAY	**Counting activities**
FRIDAY	**Visualisation activities**

Figure 7.1

Some of the activities referred to in Figure 7.1 are described in the remainder of this chapter. We hope that the activities collected here will not only support teachers in the quest for variety but also contribute to another key objective. We believe that a programme for teaching mental mathematics should include activities that will contribute to the development of the basic skills of learning. Skills of learning such as memorisation, concentration, communication, etc. will contribute to success in mental mathematics. These skills are, of course, of equal importance in all areas of the curriculum. In practice we might ask children to memorise number facts, urge them to listen carefully, or to concentrate, but we rarely offer structured advice or practice in these skills. Wood (1988) discusses the need to 'scaffold' the development of children's basic learning skills. Fisher (1995) recommends that we infuse the teaching of thinking skills into all aspects of the curriculum.

Thinking about memory

While it is important to stress that the memorisation of number facts is just a part of the agenda for mental mathematics, the value of having a 'mental toolbox' of known facts should not be underestimated. Haylock (1991) makes a strong case for developing number knowledge and sees it as one of the component parts of having confidence with number. The *Framework for Teaching Mathematics* (DfEE 1999a) suggests that facts related to all four operations should be 'known by heart' and that children should be able to 'derive quickly' a variety of other facts including number bonds, doubles and halves. Strategies to help children learn by heart or memorise facts have often been limited to the motivation provided by the desire to do well, or avoid doing badly, in regular tests. Testing remains a valid activity but it needs to be supplemented by including children in the sharing of strategies that will enhance memorisation.

Wood (1988) suggests that we would expect children to develop an awareness of the potential value of a strategic approach to memorisation as they move through the primary school. Wood reports research that shows that 5-year-olds tend to overestimate their abilities to remember when faced with the task of memorising. The children, when asked to return to a memory task in which they had achieved only limited success, showed no signs of employing a different approach to that used in their first attempt even when they had been offered examples of other strategies by an adult. Older children are able to offer far more realistic estimations of their likely performance in memory tasks. They develop an appreciation of the difficulty of memory tasks along with an awareness that a strategic approach to memorisation can enhance the chances of success. Wood suggests that learning skills such as memorisation are fostered by social interaction. In practice we would argue that once children have begun to develop an awareness of memorisation as an activity in which performance can be practised and improved, they will benefit from sharing and discussing the approaches they use and being shown potential alternative strategies by an adult.

Classic memory strategies include:

- *rehearsal* – repeatedly saying or writing a fact;
- *association* – making a connection to another image;
- *classification* – grouping, ordering or otherwise organising the information;
- *chunking* – breaking up the information to create smaller memory targets;
- *feature spotting* – identifying patterns and relationships in the information.

A common recommendation for an aid to memorisation is to personalise the information to be remembered. This approach is often called *association*. This works by creating a link between the item to be remembered and another object or event. Common advice for making associations is to make them either as bizarre or as personally significant as possible. In effect it is thought that the approach works because it is easier for us to memorise an image that we have created within our own minds than it is to capture and retain information that we merely see or hear. The identification of pattern and the classification or ordering of data are also ways in which information can be personalised.

Fisher (1995) suggests the following preferred approaches to memorising and processing information:

- *verbally* – through listening and saying or repeating information;
- *visually* – through seeing visual patterns or pictures 'in the minds eye';
- *logically* – through seeing a pattern or mathematical relation;
- *physically* – through physical representation or bodily gesture;
- *musically* – through melody, rhythm or musical association;
- *personally* – through linking information to personal experiences or memories;
- *socially* – through learning with and from others, sharing a task.

Before going on to look at some activities that should lead naturally to the development of strategies for memorisation, we would like to explore how some strategies and preferred approaches might be employed and accommodated within a specific memory task. The objective we have chosen is the memorisation of the first ten multiples of seven, or the seven times table:

$$7 \quad 14 \quad 21 \quad 28 \quad 35 \quad 42 \quad 49 \quad 56 \quad 63 \quad 70$$

- Chunking: Take out those that we know through security with the foundation tables (i.e. multiples of 1, 2, 5 and 10), and an understanding of the commutative property (i.e. $2 \times 7 = 7 \times 2$). The multiples 14, 35 and 70 can be used as reference points from which strategies such as doubling, counting on and counting back can be used.

$$7 \quad 14 \quad ? \quad ? \quad 35 \quad ? \quad ? \quad ? \quad ? \quad 70$$

- Classification: Odd and even numbers.
- Feature spotting, logically: The units digits – all are different, alternately odd and even, the square number is 1 less than 50, etc.
- Association, visually and musically: By choosing words which rhyme and suggest a mental image, e.g.

Twenty =	empty one =	bun
Thirty =	dirty two =	shoe
Forty = naughty	three = bee	
	five = hive	
	eight = plate	

so 3×7 = empty bun, 4×7 = empty plate, 5×7 = dirty hive, 6×7 = naughty shoe.

The theory behind association would suggest that the rhyming words and the consequent visual images that they imply are most likely to be useful if they are chosen by the individual who is trying to memorise the information. The imposition of this strategy would be nonsensical as it would suggest a situation in which the task is increased by adding another set of information to be memorised.

Further associations might be achieved by examining each multiple and asking for personal connections – house numbers, the day of the month we were born, the number of toys we have in a collection, etc. Building up associations for the numbers from 1 to 100 through knowing about their mathematical properties and the personal or wider cultural connotations would contribute to a genuine 'feel for number'.

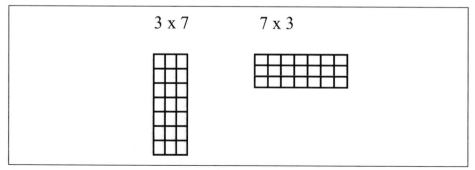

Figure 7.2

With multiplication facts a valuable visual image would be provided by arrays.

Working with arrays can contribute a number of valuable experiences and insights including:

- commutativity i.e $7 \times 8 = 8 \times 7$
- images which can be worked on for division
- visualisation of doubling and halving
- a visual image of square numbers
- an image of repeated addition when stacked or placed in a series.
- Socially: The tables might be learnt within the mathematics partnerships (see Chapter 3). At the beginning each partner could take responsibility for remembering half the facts. If tested as a pair, we might expect the added responsibility to act as a spur. The half each child is responsible for would be changed after an agreed period.

Tables tennis

- The game is played by two maths partnerships with a fifth child acting as the umpire.
- Each pair has a set of digit cards or playing cards (Ace to 10) which are placed face-down on the table (two sets of cards 1 to 10 will be enough). The cards are shuffled so that they appear randomly.
- The game focuses on multiplication.
- The multiplicand is decided before the game begins and remains the same throughout the game.
- The multipliers are provided by the cards as they are turned by the opposing pair.
- When each card is turned the opposing pair must give the product.
- The partnerships take it in turns to 'serve' five times, i.e. turn over five cards, one at a time.
- The objective (as in table tennis) is to avoid the 'ball' going out on your side of the net and avoid hitting the net as the 'ball' is returned.
- In this game the 'ball' is the question and the answers (products).
- When the multiplier card is turned, the products must be given in a certain time, e.g. five or ten seconds, or the 'ball' is out and one point goes to the serving pair.
- If the wrong product is given the 'ball' hits the net and again one point is given to the servers.
- If the product is given correctly the pair returning service score one point and the game resumes with another card being turned.
- The umpire can have the appropriate table written out and a timer.
- The pair who are returning the service can agree to take it in turns or as suggested above can concentrate on particular multipliers.

Memory activities

1. Pelmanism

- Use one suit of cards with numerals 1 to 9.
- Place them in a three-by-three array face down.
- First player turns over two cards, if they add up to 10 they are kept, if not turn them over again.
- Second player turns over one card and tries to remember if they have seen the card they need that is a complement to ten.
- The game continues until all the cards (except 5) have been removed.
- Try using two suits of 1 to 9 cards in a six-by-three array, etc.

2. Strings of five

In this exercise sets of five numbers are read out followed by a question about those numbers.

6	19	11	3	9	Which is the largest?
14	21	26	5	17	Which are even?
8	15	12	20	15	Which are multiples of 4?
2	7	9	3	1	What is the sum?

3. Collections of numbers

Choose one column of nine numbers from the set below, and explain the rules for scoring before starting.

Look at the numbers for 30 seconds. Cover them. Now write them out on a blank grid. You get two points for every number you remember and five points for every number that you put in the correct position. Be careful, you will lose 20 points if you write a number that was not there!

A		B		C		D
1		25		81		16
7		5		36		64
8		35		27		25
5		40		18		100
4		15		90		9
3		10		54		4
6		20		9		81
10		50		72		1
9		45		63		36

Figure 7.3

4. Grids

Two possible grids are as below:

1	2	3
4	5	6
7	8	9

1	2	3	4	5	6	7
8	9	10	11	12	13	14
15	16	17	18	19	20	21
22	23	24	25	26	27	28
29	30	31	32	33	34	35
36	37	38	39	40	41	42
43	44	45	46	47	48	49

Figure 7.4

Display the grid for one minute. Remove and then ask questions, e.g. as you look at the grid:
1. Which number is to the right of 19?
2. Which number is to the left of 40?
3. Which number is above 14?
4. Which number is below 22?
5. Which eight numbers surround 25?

5. Kim's game with numbers or shapes, for example:

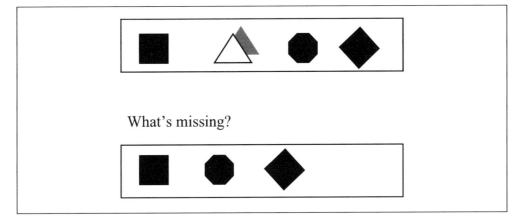

What's missing?

Figure 7.5

6. Number pairs

The pairs are selected to encourage the child to look for a relationship to help them recall the contents of the grids. For example:

2	4	6
4	8	12

16	24	32	40
8	12	16	20

3	7	9	5	4
21	49	63	35	28

Figure 7.6

The grid would be displayed for a limited period of time and then a blank grid of the same dimensions would be completed.

Listening activities

In these activities we are developing the skills of listening to and interpreting mathematical instructions. The children also have the opportunity to consolidate their mathematical vocabulary when they give the instructions. The objective of all the activities is to give a series of oral instructions so that everyone in the group ends up with the same outcome which might be a design, a pattern or a model. It is possible to base the instructions on a variety of mathematical concepts and vocabulary.

Organisation

A progression can be built into each of these activities which raises the level of challenge and introduces opportunities to practise new skills. The suggested stages would be:

Stage 1: Working together with the teacher keeping a record of the activity that can be seen by everyone in the class. After each instruction the teacher allows time for the children to respond before updating the class record so that the children can check their own versions and amend them if necessary.

Stage 2: Working together as in Stage 1 but giving more than one instruction before providing the chance to check.

Stage 3: Try to complete the whole exercise.

Stage 4: Children take over the role of giving the instructions.

Examples:
1. Coloured number tracks
Children have or make a number track 0 to 9 (see Figure 7.7) and five different

coloured crayons or pens. Teacher asks the children to colour the numbers in particular colours, e.g. colour number 3 blue, or colour the number that is one less than 6 red, or colour the number that is the sum of 3 and 5.

0	1	2	3	4	5	6	7	8	9

2. Designs in number squares (two examples)

1	2	3	4	5
6	7	8	9	10
11	12	13	14	15
16	17	18	19	20
21	22	23	24	25

1	2	3	4	5	6	7	8	9	10
11	12	13	14	15	16	17	18	19	20
21	22	23	24	25	26	27	28	29	30
31	32	33	34	35	36	37	38	39	40
41	42	43	44	45	46	47	48	49	50
51	52	53	54	55	56	57	58	59	60
61	62	63	64	65	66	67	68	69	70
71	72	73	74	75	76	77	78	79	80
81	82	83	84	85	86	87	88	89	90
91	92	93	94	95	96	97	98	99	100

Figures 7.7 and 7.8

The pupils have a grid in front of them and have to follow instructions such as: Shade in these numbers:

- the number that is two less than 15
- double 12
- half of 4
- 3 times 3
- the number that is one more than 16
- the number that is two more than 5
- double 11
- half of 24
- the number that is one less than 20
- the number of days in a week
- half of 8
- double 7.

3. Using compass points

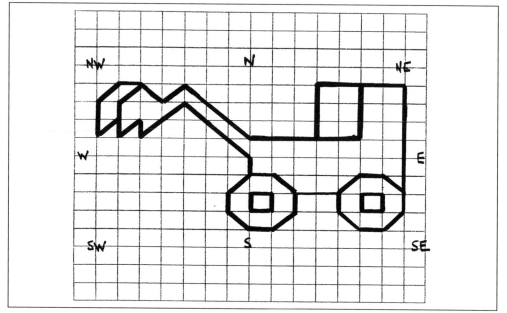

Figure 7.9

4. Grid spaces

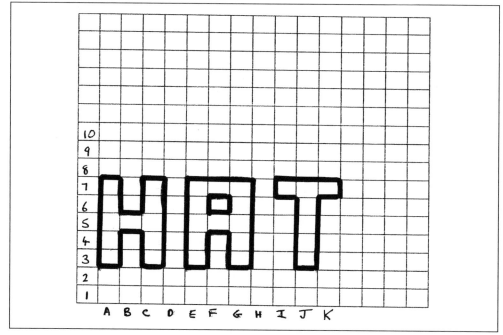

Figure 7.10

5. Co-ordinates

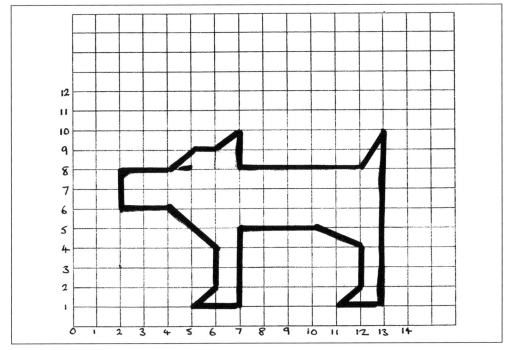

Figure 7.11

6. Follow-me games
For this activity you will need cards similar to those below:

We have 12	Follow us if you have four more
We have 16	Follow us if you have half of this
We have 8	Follow us if you have three more

   A group of pupils have a set of these cards which could be thematic – addition, subtraction, etc. Each card has two parts – the left part gives a number and the right part gives an instruction. One pupil lays down a card and whoever can follow does so. This continues until all the cards have been used.

7. Tangram designs

Give instructions to help someone position the pieces of the tangram in the arrangements shown below.

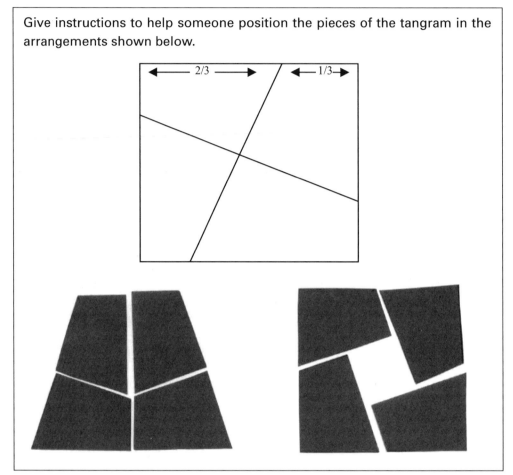

Figure 7.12

8. 3-D model building

To start the activity everyone makes an identical model with multilink cubes, e.g.:

Figure 7.13

Then cubes are added to the original model by following instructions that are given by the teacher or other children.

9. Shape relay
For this activity you need four children to work in two pairs A-B and C-D. Two of the children A and C are given a design or picture which they are going to describe to B and D respectively. They cannot name the whole design or use similes to describe it. When B has drawn a design based on the instructions of A, he or she then describes the design he or she has drawn to C and D describes the design he or she has drawn to A. (N.B. At this stage the designs that were given at the start of the activity are put to one side.) In the final pairing A describes the second design to B and C does likewise with D. At this stage it will be interesting to compare the designs that B and D have with the original designs!

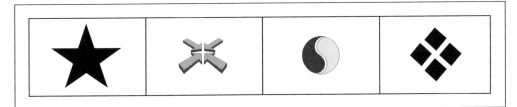

Figure 7.14

Visualisation

Hughes (1984) discovered that when 3-year-olds were asked to carry out addition and subtraction problems they could often provide the correct answer when the problem was linked to a game in which bricks were added to and taken away from a box. The box was closed when the children were asked to calculate how many bricks were inside, which meant that the option to count the bricks by direct one-to-one correspondence was not open to them. It seems likely that many of the children would have made the link between the abstracted number problem and the concrete representation provided by the bricks by visualising the bricks and counting them as they appeared in the mental image. In Chapter 4 we referred to images of number that we feel could underpin a child's ability to carry out mental calculation. We made the distinction between reference tools, e.g. standard number lines and number squares, and thinking tools such as the blank number line. These images can only be used in mental mathematics if the child can visualise them. The work of Hughes (1984) would suggest that the skill of visualisation is an ability that develops automatically in response to stimuli. Taking the position argued by Wood (1988) in respect of memory we suggest that visualisation should be viewed as an activity and that visual competence can be accelerated by providing structured and regular exercise. Some examples of appropriate exercises are as follows.

1. Stories

Close your eyes (we might expect this to cut down on distraction!). I am going to describe a picture in which something is happening. I want you to try to imagine the picture I am describing and then I am going to ask you some questions about what you saw in your mind's eye.

There are five rabbits, they are all wearing hats, the hats have holes in them so that their ears stick through. Even stranger they are all riding bicycles. They are riding along a path which is at the top of a bank. We are standing at the bottom of the bank looking up at them as they ride along. Behind the rabbits we can see just sky. The rabbit that is third takes his paws off the handlebars and rides along shouting to the others to look. Then he starts to wobble. He falls off and the rabbits who were behind him, fourth and fifth in the row, crash into him and fall off as well.

- How many are left on their bikes?
- How many fell off?
- What did their hats look like? What sort of hats did they have?
- Were they wearing other clothes? What were they wearing? etc.

The answers to the last two questions will help establish that everyone may have seen things differently.

2. Words

- Imagine the word *table* written directly above the word *water*.
- Which letter is under the letter b?
- Which letter is above the letter r? etc.

3. Cutting cube arrays

- Imagine 24 multilink cubes.
- They are arranged into columns of six.
- How many columns are there?
- We glue them into a block.
- We are going to take a very sharp knife and cut them into three equal pieces.
- Imagine where you cut and tell me how many cubes are in each piece.

4. Framework 3-D shapes

- We are going to build a climbing frame and then climb on it and move around.

- The climbing frame is going to be a cube.
- There is a pile of strong cylindrical plastic poles. Just enough to make a cube. How many are there?
- Four of the poles have hand- or foot-holds sticking out of them on two sides. Where are you going to put them?
- Four of the poles are wider than the others and have a flat side that is wide enough to make it easier to balance on them. Where will you use these?
- There are some joints. Just enough to make a cube. How many?
- The joints have holes in them that the poles fit in. What do you think they might look like?
- Draw one. How many holes do they have in them?
- Put the climbing frame together.
- Before we climb onto it we need to put some pegs in to keep it fixed to the ground. The pegs are like 'U's and we hammer them into the ground so that the poles that are lying flat on the ground can't move. There are 20 pegs and we should put the same number along each pole that is lying on the ground. How many do we put on each pole?
- You are going to climb now.
- You walk along one bottom edge.
- At the corner you turn and walk along another bottom edge.
- Then you turn and climb up a vertical edge to a top corner.
- Then you walk, carefully, along one of the top horizontal edges.
- Then you remember that you left your sweets at the point that you started.
- How many edges do you need to walk along to get back to them?

5. Plasticine shapes

- Imagine a cube made of plasticine.
- It is balanced on one of its vertices on a table top.
- You take a very sharp knife and cut through the cube, horizontally just above the vertex which is touching the table.
- You remove the small piece that you have cut from the cube.
- What shape is the new face that the cube has?
- What shape is the bit you cut off?
- How many faces does the cube have now?
- How many edges?
- How many vertices?

6. Number tracks

- We have 11 big carpet squares.
- They have the numbers 0, 1, 2, 3, 4, 5, 6, 7, 8, 9 and 10 written on them.
- We put them in the right order in a path so that 0 is nearest to us and 10 is furthest away.
- I want you to imagine that you are walking along the carpet squares.
- I will tell you which number you start on and then I will tell you how many squares to walk either forwards or backwards.
- Stand on 0, walk forward 4. Which number are you standing on?
- Stand on 4, walk forward 2. Which number are you standing on? etc.

7. 100 squares

- We are standing on a giant 100 square. It starts at 0 and ends at 99.
- I want you to imagine that you are walking on the square.
- I will tell you which number you start on and then I will tell you how many squares to walk either up, down, left or right.
- Start at 25 and go up one square. Which number are you standing on? etc.
- Increase to two instructions and three instructions, etc.
- Introduce diagonal moves.

8. The Borrowers' multilink models

Imagine that you are a Borrower, a tiny person; a multilink cube is twice as tall as you. You are going to investigate some models made of multilink and work out how many cubes are used in each model. This is an example:

The first model. The wall you look at is four cubes wide and two cubes high. There is a ladder against the wall and you climb up. When you get to the top you can see that the rest of the model is only one cube high. It is all four cubes wide and you can see four more rows of cubes, apart from the row that you are standing on. How many cubes are there altogether in this model?

Elimination activities

We are recommending that a range of different formats would be used for the warm-up activities of the daily mathematics lesson. Formats for whole-class interactive sessions which are flexible enough to be used throughout the primary school and therefore are familiar to both teachers and children will cut down the time needed for introductions and preparation. Elimination games provide one example of a versatile format. The objective for all of these games is to find one item that has been selected by the teacher (or child who is leading the activity) from a known group of items (e.g. numbers 1 to 10, 1 to 100 or 16 shapes). The item is found by using clues which enable the player to eliminate some of the possibilities.

An essential ingredient (to enable all children to participate) is for individuals or pairs of children to keep a record of what is being eliminated after each piece of information is given and that there should be a class record, that everyone can see, which is updated after each turn. The shared record means that children can check their own records and that reasons for decisions they have made can be explored and explained. Children may also be able to identify patterns and describe features they have found which speeds up the recording process (e.g. when eliminating all the odd numbers on a 1 to 100 square they may start by examining each number separately, but it is likely that someone will see a shortcut and that discovery/knowledge can be shared). Below are examples of elimination games for all ages.

Number lines 0 to 10

- The children make their own 0 to 10 number tracks or use counters to cover tracks that are provided.
- There will be a big number track that everyone can see and which is updated after each clue (i.e. after a pause for the children to choose which number has been referred to in each clue).

Clues can be given at three levels of difficulty as shown below:

1. By association or counting, e.g. it is not the number of times I am going to clap my hands; it is not the number of sides a triangle has.
2. Using the language of more than/less than, e.g. the number I am thinking of is not one more than 3 … one less than 7, etc.
3. Using calculations, e.g. the number I am thinking of is not the sum of 2 and 3.

Keywords could be displayed so that they can be read by the whole class.

In elimination activities questions could be provided to help all the children participate in an activity:

odd	Is it odd/even ?
even	
greater than	Is it greater than/less than …?
less than	
multiple of	Is it a multiple of …?
digit	Presence of a digit, e.g. does it have a 3?
	Is the tens digit bigger than the units digit? etc.

prime	Is it prime?
factor	Is (e.g. 5) a factor of the number?
difference between	Is the difference between the digits greater than ...?

The teacher starts the activity by saying:

'I am thinking of a number between 1 and 100 and you must try to find out what the number is. You can ask questions that can be answered yes or no. After each answer you can eliminate the numbers that it cannot be. In this game I will not answer the same sort of question twice, for example, you can only use "more than" in one question. Some example questions are in the keyword box. Before we start let's have a look at the keywords. Can you remind us what the word *prime* means? Y ... How about *factor*, etc.'

- Start the questions.

After each question the children are allowed some time to eliminate numbers from their squares and then either a volunteer or the teacher updates the class record.

- Invite children to show you any patterns they can see.
- Continue until only one number remains.
- When the activity is familiar, children can choose a number and field the questions.

Estimation

The following activities are all designed to help the pupils develop the skill of estimating.

1. Pick 'em ups

Use a variety of objects of a size that allows several to be picked up with one hand simultaneously, e.g. counters, multilink, rubbers, pencils.

- Ask the children to guess how many you can pick up in one hand.
- Ask them how many a child will be able to pick up.

2. Which of the answers must be wrong and how do you know?

162 +79 121	162 +79 521	162 +79 81	162 +79 241	162 +79 235

3. Best guess

Which of the three possible answers is correct? How did you know?

7.2 x 9.8	52.16	98.36	70.56
1200 x 0.89	722	1068	131
313 x 107.6	3642.8	4281.8	33678.8
6.72 ☐ 0.12	6.32	21.2	56
0.143 ☐ 0.11	2.3	1.3	11.4

4. Estimating measures

In the same way that personal approaches to mental arithmetic provide the foundation for a 'feel for number' the ability to estimate is the bedrock for the development of a 'feel for measurement'. Research also tells us that the analogy extends to the way arithmetic and measurement is used in the real world, i.e. that mental calculation is far more common than the use of formal written algorithms and it is far more common for us to estimate rather than measure accurately.

APU (Assessment Performance Unit) studies (1991) provide evidence that, while the calculation of volume and area by use of formula rates among the most common experiences offered in the mathematics curriculum, measurement using practical apparatus and estimation are rated among the five least common experiences. The same study noted that success rates in tests on estimation skills were uniformly low.

Exercises in estimating in all systems of measurement can be run as whole-class mental activities. A progression in such tasks would begin with comparing two lengths, weights, capacities, etc. to suggest which is the longer, heavier and would hold the most. Extending the task to three items and more and asking for them to be ordered could be the next stage.

Skills in estimation will depend on the establishment of reference points for each system of measurement. For example, we might base estimates of capacity by comparing containers to a drinks can which holds about 330 ml or $\frac{1}{3}$ of a litre. 30 cm rulers and metre rules can provide experiential reference points for linear measurement. To help establish reference points activities which ask the child to group items into those that would, for example, weigh more than and less than one kilogram might prove helpful.

Regular challenges to estimate measures can be used throughout the key stages with older children calculating margins of error to score their performance.

Endnote

Throughout the book we have tried to merge theory and practice, so that in each chapter the activities suggested are preceded by a discussion of the relevant research issues. We hope that in this way the activities are put in context and seen as more than something that the pupils will enjoy doing. Naturally it is our wish that not only will both teacher and pupil enjoy exploring at least some of the activities within the book but also that the context and learning opportunities are clear. We strongly support the present emphasis on mental mathematics and we feel that the material within this book will help to enhance the opportunities that can be offered to the pupils for pursuing a range of mental strategies. Thus rather than offering a collection of "one off" activities it has been our intention to provide examples of how the lessons of research can be translated into a programme for mental mathematics.

Bibliography

Alexander, R. J. (1991) *Primary Education in Leeds: Twelfth and Final Report from the Primary Needs Project.* Leeds: University of Leeds.

Alexander, R. J. (1997) *Policy and Practice in Primary Education: Local Initiative, National Agenda.* London: Routledge.

Alexander, R. J., Rose, A. J., Woodhead, C. (1992) *Curriculum Organisation and Classroom Practice in Primary Schools, a Discussion Paper.* London: DES.

Anghileri, J. (1991) 'The language of multiplication and division', in Durkin, K. and Shire, B. (eds) *Language in Mathematical Education.* Buckingham: Open University Press.

Anghileri, J. (1995) 'Use of counting in multiplication and division', in Thompson, F. I. (ed.) *Teaching and Learning Early Number.* Buckingham: Open University Press.

Anghileri, J. (1997) *Making Sense of Symbols in Children's Mathematical Thinking in the Primary Years.* London: Cassell.

Askew, M. *et al.* (1997) *Effective Teachers of Numeracy.* London: King's College.

Askew, M. (1998) *Teaching Primary Mathematics.* London: Hodder & Stoughton.

Assessment and Performance Unit (APU) (1991) *APU Mathematics Monitoring (Phase 2).* London: SEAC.

Association for Teachers of Mathematics (ATM) (1997) *Mathematics Teaching 160.* Derby: Association of Teachers of Mathematics.

Atkinson, S. (ed.) (1991) *Mathematics with Reason.* London: Hodder & Stoughton.

Basic Skills Agency (1997) *International Numeracy Survey: A comparison of the basic numeracy skills of adults 16–60 in seven countries.* The Basic Skills Agency.

Bierhoff, H. (1996) *Laying the Foundations for Numeracy.* London: ESRC.

Botsmanova, M. E. (1972) 'The forms of pictorial aid in arithmetic problem solving', in Kirkpatrick, J. and Wirzsup, I. (eds) *Soviet Studies in the Psychology of Learning and Teaching Mathematics.* Vol. vi, pp. 105–10. Chicago: University of Chicago Press.

Brousseau, G. (1997) *Theory of Didactical Situations in Mathematics.* The Netherlands: Kluwer Academic Publishers.

Bruce, T. (1991) *Time to Play in Early Childhood Education.* London: Hodder & Stoughton.

Bruner, J. S. (1964) 'Some theorems on instruction illustrated with reference to mathematics', in *Theories of Learning and Instruction*, NSSE Yearbook. Chicago: NSSE.

Bruner, J. S. (1970) 'Some theorems on instruction in readings', in *Educational Psychology*, Stones, E. (ed.) London: Methuen.

Campbell, P. (1981) 'What do children seen in textbook pictures?', *Arithmetic Teacher* **59**(2), pp. 12–16.

Cobb, P. *et al.* (1992) 'A constructivist alternative to the representational view of mind in mathematics education', in *Journal for Research in Mathematics Education*, **23**(1), pp. 2–33.

Cobb, P. *et al.* (1995) 'Learning through problem-solving: a constructivist approach to second grade mathematics', in Murphy, P. (ed.) *Subject Learning in the Primary School.* Milton Keynes: Open University Press.

Cockroft, W. H. (1982) *Mathematics Counts: Report of the Committee of Inquiry into the Teaching of Mathematics in Schools.* London: HMSO.

Coulby, D. and Ward, S. (1996) *The Primary Core National Curriculum.* London: Cassell.

Croll, P. and Moses, D. (1985) *One in Five: The Assessment and Incidence of Special Educational Needs.* London: Routledge & Kegan Paul.

Davis, A. (1991) 'Piaget, teachers, and education: into the 1990s', in Light, P. *et al.* (ed.) *Learning to Think.* London: Routledge.

Davydov, V. V. (1991) 'A psychological analysis of multiplication', in *Psychological Abilities of Primary School Children in Learning Mathematics.* Virginia: NCTM.

DfEE (1998a) *Numeracy Matters: The Preliminary Report of the Numeracy Task Force.* London: DfEE.

DfEE (1998b) *The Implementation of the National Numeracy Strategy: The Final Report of the Numeracy Task Force.* London: DfEE.

DfEE (1999a) *The National Numeracy Strategy: Framework for Teaching Mathematics.* London: DfEE.

DfEE (1999b) *National Curriculum Review Consultation.* London: DfEE.

DfEE (1999c) The National Numeracy Strategy: Two-day course for leading mathematics teachers. Overhead projector transparencies. London: DfEE.

DfEE (1999d) *The National Numeracy Strategy: Mathematics Vocabulary.* London: DfEE.

DfEE (1999e) *The National Curriculum.* London: DfEE.

Duchastel S. and Waller B. (1979) 'Pictorial illustrations in instructional texts', in *Educational Technology* **19**, pp. 20–25.

Ernest, P. (1991) *The Philosophy of Mathematics Education.* London: Falmer Press.

Ernest, P. (1994) 'What is social constructivism', in *Proceedings of the 18th International Conference on the Psychology of Mathematics Education.* Portugal.

Faux, G. (1998) 'What are the big ideas in mathematics?', *Mathematics Teaching* (MT 163). Derby: Association of Teachers of Mathematics.

Faux, G. (1999) *Gattegno Charts.* Carlisle: Education Initiatives.

Feilker, D. (1997) 'Some notes on mental mathematics', *Mathematics Teaching 160.* Derby: Association of Teachers of Mathematics.

Filloy, E. and Sutherland, R. (1996) 'Algebra', in Kilpatrick, J. (ed.) *International Handbook of Mathematics Education.* The Netherlands: Kluwer Academic Publishers.

Fischbein E. *et al* (1985) 'The role of implicit models in solving verbal problems in multiplication and division'. *Journal of Research in Mathematics Education* **16** 3–17.

Fisher, R. (1995) *Teaching Children to Learn.* Cheltenham: Stanley Thornes.

Floyd, A. (ed.) (1981) *Developing Mathematical Thinking.* London: Addison-Wesley/Open University Press.

Galton, M. (1998) *Reliving the ORACLE Experience: Back to Basics or Back to the Future?* University of Warwick: Centre for Research in Elementary and Primary Education.

Galton, M. and Simon, B. (eds) (1980) *Progress and Performance in the Primary Classroom.* London: Routledge & Kegan Paul.

Galton, M. and Wilcocks, J. (eds) (1983) *Moving from the Primary Classroom.* London: Routledge & Kegan Paul.

Glaserfeld, E. von (1987) 'Learning as a constructive activity', in Janvier, C. (ed.) *Problems of Representation in the Teaching and Learning of Mathematics.* Hillsdale: LEA Publishers.

Glaserfeld, E. von (1995) *Radical Constructivism.* London: Falmer Press.

Goulding, M. (1992) 'Examining assumptions', *Micromath* **8**(3), pp. 38–9.

Gravemeijer, K. (1994) *Developing Realistic Mathematics.* Culemborg, The Netherlands: Technipress.

Gray, E. and Tall, D. (1993) 'Duality, ambiguity and flexibility: a perceptual view of simple arithmetic', *Journal for Research in Mathematics Education* **25**(2), pp. 116–40.

Harel, I. and Papert, S. (1991) *Constructionism.* Norwood, NJ: Ablex Publications.

Harlen W. (1992) *The Teaching of Science.* London: David Fulton Publishers.

Harries, A.V. (1997) 'Reflections on a Hungarian mathematics lesson', *Mathematics Teaching* (MT 162). Derby: Association of Teachers of Mathematics.

Harries, T. and Sutherland. R. (1998) *A Comparison of Primary Mathematics Text Books from Five Countries with a particular Focus on the Treatment of Number.* Unpublished QCA Report. University of Bristol, Graduate School of Education, Bristol.

Harries, T. and Sutherland, R. (1999) 'Primary school mathematics text books: an international comparison', in Thompson, I. (ed.) *Issues in Teaching Numeracy in Primary Schools.* Oxford: Open University Press.

Haylock, D. (1991) *Mathematics Explained for Primary Teachers.* London: Paul Chapman Publishing.

Holt, D. (1984) *How Children Fail.* London: Penguin.

Howe M. J. A. (1992) *The Origins of Exceptional Ability.* Oxford: Basil Blackwell.

Hughes, M. (1984) *Children and Numbers.* London: Hodder & Stoughton.

Jaworski, B. (1994) *Investigating Mathematics Teaching*. London: Falmer Press.

Johnson, D. (ed.) (1984) *Children's Mathematical Frameworks 8–13: A Study of Classroom Teaching*. Reading: NFER-Nelson.

Kaput, J. (1991) 'Notations and representations as mediators of constructive processes', in von Glaserfeld, E. (ed.) *Radical Constructivism in Mathematics Education*. The Netherlands: Kluwer Academic Publishers.

Krutetski, V. A. (1976) *The Psychology of Mathematical Abilities in School Children*. Chicago: University of Chicago Press.

Light, P. *et al.* (eds) (1991) *Learning to Think*. London: Routledge.

Lins, R. (1992) *A Framework for Understanding what Algebraic Thinking is*. Unpublished PhD thesis. University of Nottingham.

LMS, IMA, RSS (1995) *Tackling the Mathematics Problem*. London: The London Mathematical Society.

MacDonald, F. J. (1964) 'The influence of learning theories on education', in *Theories of Learning and Instruction*, NSSE Yearbook. Chicago: NSSE.

McIntosh, A. (1977) 'When will they ever learn?', in Floyd, A. (ed.) (1981) *Developing Mathematical Thinking*. London: Addison-Wesley/Open University Press.

Measor, L. and Woods, P. (1984) *Changing Schools: Pupil Perspectives on Transfer to a Comprehensive*. Milton Keynes: Open University Press.

Millett, A. and Askew, M. (1994) 'Teachers' perceptions of using and applying mathematics', *Mathematics Teacher* **148**, pp. 3–7.

Mortimore, P. *et al.* (1987) *School Matters: The Junior Years*. London: Open Books.

Mullis, I. V. S. *et al.* (1997) *Mathematics Achievement in the Primary School Years: IEA's Third Mathematics and Science Study*. Massachusetts: Boston College.

National Curriculum Council (NCC) (1989) *Mathematics Non-statutory Guidance*. London: HMSO.

Nickson, M. and Lerman, S. (eds) (1992) *The Social Context of Mathematics Education: Theory and Practice*. London: Southbank Press.

Nunes, T. and Bryant, P. (1996) *Children Doing Mathematics*. Oxford: Blackwell.

OFSTED (1993a) *Mathematics Key Stages 1, 2 & 3*. London: HMSO.

OFSTED (1993b) *The Teaching and Learning of Number in the Primary School*. London: HMSO.

Ollerenshaw, C. and Ritchie, R. (1993) *Primary Science: Making it Work*, 2nd edn. London: David Fulton Publishers.

Osborn, S. *et al.* (1996) *Being a Pupil in England and France: Findings from a Comparative Study*. Paper presented at the 17th Comparative Education Society in Europe Conference, Athens.

Papert, S. (1972) 'Teaching children to be mathematicians versus teaching about mathematics', *International Journal of Mathematics Education in Science and Technology* **3**, pp. 249–62.

Piaget, J. (1969) 'Advances in child and adolescent psychology', in *Science of Education and the Psychology of the Child*. Harlow: Longman.

Pollard, A. *et al.* (1994) *Changing English Primary Schools? The Impact of the Education Reform Act at Key Stage One.* London: Cassell.

Popper K. R. (1979) *Objective Knowledge, (revised edn).* Oxford: Oxford University Press.

Rees, R. and Barr, G. (1984) *Diagnosis and Prescription.* London: Harper and Row.

Resnick, L. B. and Ford, W. W. (1981) *The Psychology of Mathematics for Instruction.* London: LEA.

Rowe, M. B. (1986). 'Wait-times: slowing down may be a way of speeding up!', *Journal of Teacher Education* 37, pp. 43–50.

Santos-Bernard, D. (1997) *The Use of Illustrations in School Mathematics Text Books – Presentation of Information.* Unpublished PhD thesis. University of Nottingham.

Sewell, B. (1981) *Use of Mathematics by Adults in Daily Life.* London: Advisory Council for Adult and Continuing Education (ACACE).

Shuard, H. and Rothery, A. (1988) *Children Reading Mathematics.* London: John Murray.

Smith, A. (1996) *Accelerated Learning in the Classroom.* Stafford: Network Educational Press.

Steffe, L. P. (1994) 'Children's multiplying schemes', in Harel, G. and Confrey, J. (eds) *The Development of Multiplicative Reasoning in the Learning of Mathematics.* Albany, NY: State University of New York Press.

Straker, A. (1993) *Talking Point in Mathematics.* Cambridge: Cambridge University Press.

Stones, E. (1966) *An Introduction to Educational Psychology.* London: Methuen.

Tall, D. (1993) 'The transition from arithmetic to algebra: number patterns or proceptual programming', in *Proceedings of Second Annual Conference On Teaching and Learning.* London: Institute of Education.

Tall, D. (1996) 'Can all children climb the same curriculum ladder?', in *The Mathematical Ability of School Leavers.* Gresham Special Lecture, Gresham College, London.

Tall, D. and Gray, E. (1993) 'Success and failure in mathematics', in *Mathematics Teaching* (MT 142). pp. 6–10. Derby: Association of Teachers of Mathematics.

Tharp, R. and Gallimore, R. (1991) 'A theory of learning as assisted performance', in Light, P. *et al.* (eds) *Learning to Think.* Oxford: Routledge.

Vanlehn, K. (1990) *Mindbugs.* Boston, Mass: MIT Press.

Vergnaud, G. (1982) 'Cognitive and developmental psychology and research in mathematical education: some theoretical and methodological issues', in *For the Learning of Mathematics* 3(2), pp. 31–41. Montreal, Canada

Vergnaud, G. (1984) 'Problem-solving and symbolism in the development of mathematical concepts', in *Proceedings of the International Conference on the Psychology of Mathematics Education.* Sydney, Australia.

Vergnaud, G. (1990) 'Problem-solving and concept formation in the learning of mathematics', in *Learning and Instruction* 2(2), Mandl *et al.* (eds) London: Pergammon Press.

Vygotsky, L. (1978) *Mind in Society.* Cambridge, Mass: Harvard University Press.

Wood, D. (1988) *How Children Think and Learn.* Oxford: Blackwell.

Index